BEING
INDISPENSABLE

BEING
INDISPENSABLE

A School Librarian's Guide to Becoming an Invaluable Leader

Ruth Toor and Hilda K. Weisburg

American Library Association
Chicago 2011

While extensive effort has gone into ensuring the reliability of the information in this book, the publisher makes no warranty, express or implied, with respect to the material contained herein.

⊗ This paper meets the requirements of ANSI/NISO Z39.48-1992 (Permanence of Paper).

Library of Congress Cataloging-in-Publication Data
Toor, Ruth, 1933-
  Being indispensable : a school librarian's guide to becoming an invaluable leader / Ruth Toor and Hilda K. Weisburg.
      p.   cm.
  Includes bibliographical references and index.
  ISBN 978-0-8389-1065-8 (alk. paper)
  1. School libraries—United States—Administration. 2. Instructional materials centers United States—Administration. 3. School libraries—Aims and objectives. 4. School libraries—Public relations. 5. School libraries—Evaluation. 6. Leadership. I. Weisburg, Hilda K., 1942- II. Title.
  Z675.S3T5847 2011
  025.1'978—dc22

                                                                                    2010014055

ISBN: 978-0-8389-1065-8

Printed in the United States of America
15 14   5 4 3

Cover design by Karen Sheets de Gracia
Illustrations by Jill Davis
Text design in Shannon and Sabon by Kirstin Krutsch

Ruth Toor is a consultant after retiring from her job of twenty-nine years as the school librarian at Southern Boulevard School in Chatham, N.J. Having been president of the American Association of School Librarians (AASL) and a member of ALA Council, she still works actively on ALA, AASL, and ALSC committees. During her AASL presidency, she was its representative to the National Forum for History Standards and helped critique the National Social Studies and English/Language Arts Standards. She was also a member of the Implementation Committee for *Information Power: Building Partnerships for Learning,* the former AASL National Standards. She is an Internship Adviser for Professional Development Studies at Rutgers University's School of Communication and Information. She was honored with the President's Award as well as the Lifetime Membership Award of the New Jersey Association of School Librarians (NJASL). She earned her BA at the University of Delaware—where she was inducted into the Alumni Wall of Fame—and her MLS at Rutgers.

Hilda Weisburg retired as library media specialist at Morristown High School in Morristown, N.J., in 2004. She has taught graduate courses at William Paterson University and Rutgers University. A past president of NJASL, she is the association's delegate to AASL's Affiliate Assembly, on which she has served as chair and Region II director. Currently, she is a member of the ALA Literacy Committee and the ALA/CBC (Children's Book Council) Joint Committee. She is the chair of the 2010 National Institute (Fall Forum). She has given presentations at AASL and state library media conferences and given staff development workshops for many school districts. In addition, she has been a library consultant for several New Jersey districts. With Ruth Toor, she has written thirteen books for librarians, the most recent being *New on the Job: A School Library Media Specialist's Guide to Success.* The duo has been writing and editing the *School Librarian's Workshop* since 1980.

CONTENTS

INTRODUCTION

Why did we write *Being Indispensable*? Primarily, it was to raise awareness that twenty-first-century learning *requires* school librarians to be leaders. The world has changed, and what you do has become more critical than ever. However, too many school librarians have not been proactive in their buildings, and there has been an ongoing disconnect between what *you* know you do and what administrators and teachers think you do.

This lack of understanding, especially in an economic downturn, has led to severe cuts and elimination of positions. Many wonder if school librarians have become an endangered species. You no longer have an option about becoming an indispensable building leader. Your students and your job depend on it.

Our previous book, *New on the Job*, covered the basics that every school librarian should master in order to be comfortable and successful. *Being Indispensable* is the advanced course. Keeping your job, particularly in tough times, requires a deeper understanding and a commitment to doing it better—and differently. By following these suggestions and recommendations, you can become so invaluable that no one would consider eliminating your position.

Think of this text as a cookbook. You never use all the recipes. Choose those ideas that interest you the most, and begin implementing your plan for success.

Being Indispensable is about leadership and advocacy as well as about knowing and modeling the latest educational trends. Instead of obsessing about why your very small piece of the educational world is not working and you deserve better, you need to have compassion and empathy for all your colleagues from the top down—from superintendent to custodian—and recognize that everyone is struggling and having a hard time and that you are not their personal target.

However, you can do everything in this book and do it well and still find your job in jeopardy. Sometimes a decision is made at a higher level by people who don't know what you are doing no matter how much you are respected in your building. Sometimes budgets have shrunk so much that there is really no alternative for the school board. You may still be able to save your job, however, even under these dire circumstances, if you have mastered advocacy and built a strong base of support. In large districts where remote superintendents make decisions, principals can have tremendous authority for their own buildings regarding how their budget will be spent, thereby saving your job. You can see that you have many options. Be sure to check the web resources in the appendix for further help.

Best wishes to you in weathering this crisis as you learn to be even more efficient, effective, and indispensable!

PART I
Knowing Who You Are

Before you can become indispensable, you must develop a clear picture of who you are and what you do. You will be promoting yourself and your program, so it is imperative that you know exactly what that means. In the next three chapters you will go through an extended process to ensure that you are ready to weave yourself into the fabric of the educational community. The more tightly you do so, the more difficult it will be to remove you without damaging the whole.

In chapter 1 you identify what is unique about you and your role, create a compelling mission statement, and ground yourself in a philosophy that will sustain and empower you. Borrowing from the corporate world, you will learn how to brand your program in a way that keeps the *most* essential aspects of it front and center in everyone's mind.

Chapter 2 challenges you to recognize the professional and personal qualities that make a good leader. You must be aware of them all and know how to draw on them to become a force within your building or district or both. You will learn how to leverage both the National Educational Technology Standards (NETS) and the AASL *Standards for the 21st-Century Learner*.

The third chapter guides you in using what you have learned in the preceding chapters to prepare two related strategic plans. The first plan is a personal one in which you set goals and develop action plans for positioning yourself as an invaluable building leader and asset to the educational community. The second plan is for positioning your program to make it a part of every classroom. Last, you learn how to manage your time effectively so that you can get everything accomplished without feeling constantly overwhelmed.

CHAPTER 1
What's Your Mission?

You are a conscientious school librarian. You love your job and your students. On the whole, you enjoy working with your colleagues. Yet you have begun to wonder if your position is secure. Is there a way to become indispensable?

Welcome to Reality 101. Having a place on the organizational chart of a district or being tenured is no guarantee that your program—and you—won't be eliminated. Everything is subject to change. Although this has always been true to some degree, tough economic times exacerbate the problem.

Everywhere, administrators are confronted by difficult decisions. Whether the state or federal government requires that new competencies be included or budget shortfalls demand that programs and staff be cut, the ax will fall somewhere. Who goes and who stays depends on their perceived value.

Not generally recognized by those outside it, the school community is a hodgepodge of overlapping tasks and responsibilities. Classroom teachers, literacy coaches, reading teachers, and school librarians all affect students' ability and interest in reading. Teachers, computer specialists, and school librarians must ensure that students choose and use technology at a twenty-first-century level. Hard-pressed superintendents, looking only at the surface, can easily decide that the school librarian is redundant.

Your ongoing challenge is to demonstrate at all times that what you and your school library program (SLP) provide is central to achieving the essential goals of the district and that students will be harmed if they are deprived of what they learn in the school library under the directions of a skilled, certificated school librarian. You do this by accepting that it is up to *you* to get this message out, repeating it clearly and consistently and demonstrating it in everything you do.

If you are not one already, you must become a building (and perhaps a district) leader. You have to know what is going on *outside* the school library and how that activity might impact your program. Advocacy skills need to be cultivated and honed and relationships developed. It is a tall order, and it begins with knowing who you are and what your position is within the school community.

CLAIM YOUR TERRITORY

Begin with a mental exercise to define your territory. Be careful—this is just a thinking process to get you started. You *never* want to be seen as guarding your turf or protecting it no matter what else is happening in the district. However, you *do* want to identify the segment of the school program that is uniquely yours. What place does the SLP have relative to reading and literacy? What does it do with technology not covered anywhere else? What *more* do you contribute to preparing students for the twenty-first century and improving student achievement?

According to the first Common Belief in AASL's *Standards for the 21st-Century Learner,* "Reading is a window to the world."[1] The SLP keeps that window open by bringing the joy rather than focusing on the lesson. You interact with students so that all of them can find and access material in print and other formats, illuminating that world and "develop[ing] new understandings." As a result, and through sharing their enjoyment with others or treasuring it for themselves, they become lifelong readers. Knowing *how* to read does not create a habit. Deriving pleasure from reading makes students as well as adults want to continue the practice.

Although specific technology skills may be addressed in a curriculum, from the students' perspective these tools are a natural part of their environment. If they perceive a tool as important to them, they learn how to use it on their own, as they have for everything from video games to iPods. In the SLP, using a database or creating a podcast should *not* be the purpose of a lesson. These are merely resources to be employed as part of the complete research process, which includes sharing as much as locating information. As students discover the value of the sources and, through your guidance, become skilled at evaluating the credibility of online information, they apply this knowledge to their personal searches. Their experiences in the school library prepare them to become global citizens, proficient in an ever-changing, technology-based environment.

In going through this process of defining your territory, list words and phrases that make the most sense to you. Add others that you find important or significant. Be sure that whatever you list is equally valuable to the administration. It does not matter how important *you* think an activity is. Your program will be supported only to the extent that those holding the purse strings see how it benefits *their* goals.

Your Unique Contributions

List at least three activities or benefits exclusive to the SLP.

1. _____

2. _____

3. _____

WRITE A MISSION STATEMENT

A mission statement clearly identifies your purpose, your reason for being "in business," proclaiming your objective to all who enter your facility or come in contact with your program. As such, the mission statement must be succinct, easily understandable (free of library terminology), and of significance to a broad audience. Most important, it must be visible—not merely words posted on a website but rather a living, breathing reminder of what the SLP does for students and staff *every single day.*

In addition to telling everyone what you do, a mission statement helps clarify your priorities. When making choices of what you should or should not be doing or where to put your emphasis, consider what you have said is your purpose. Does this action or task promote or take away from that purpose? For example, if lifelong reading is not part of your mission statement, you should not place a high priority on purchasing books and magazines for recreational reading. Think carefully about what is and is not a highly important aspect of your program. Once this statement is universally accepted in your building, you can use it as a communication tool for explaining to a teacher why plopping students in front of computers to complete a rote assignment without any guidance or direction from you is not making the best use of what the SLP offers.

The mental exercise you completed in claiming your territory gives you the basis for writing your statement. You can also turn to the AASL Standards and to *Empowering Learners: Guidelines for School Library Media Programs*[2] to be sure your statement is aligned with the national organization's guidelines. Once you have a very rough draft, examine what you wrote to be sure you are not using terminology understood only by fellow school librarians.

Information literacy skills may not be the same to an administrator as they are to you. For example, the term *fluency* is now being used more than *literacy* in educational circles. Educators also prefer the term *information and communication technology* (ICT). Indeed, the Educational Testing Service (www.ets .org), producer of the well-known SATs, has an i-Skills[3] exam on ICT at two levels. The basic level is for students moving to a four-year college or those in their first two years of college. The Partnership for 21st Century Skills (www .p21.org)[4] includes the category Information, Media, and Technology Skills in its framework. So, as you write, test your language with others outside the school library to be sure you are being understood.

Before going on to the next section, do a rough draft of your mission statement. There is plenty of time to revise, tinker, and tweak. Focus on what you consider your chief purpose. Refer to what you said is unique about your program. Think of twenty-first-century skills that are your responsibility to teach. Keep in mind that you are speaking to everyone who comes into your library. When your mission statement is completed, you not only post it on your website but print it out, frame it, and hang it on the wall.

Finally, remember the statement must be brief and to the point. Your target should be about twenty-five words (definitely under fifty) not including the opening sentence: "The mission of the _____ School Library Program is . . . " Be sure to write in the present tense.

Sample Mission Statements

Students in courses and participants in workshops have created mission statements for their programs, and some of those statements are reproduced in this section. Many are based on the now superseded *Information Power: Building Partnerships for Learning.*[5] Some are too long; none should be taken as perfect. They are here to show you the different ways you can write your statement and what you might include.

Now that you have gotten started, review the following examples. Select phrases you like and rework what you have done. Watch out for words like *support* or *enrich*. These are red-flag phrases. In a pinch, administrators can do away with a program that does either. Instead, choose a word like *integral*.

- The _____ School District Library Program promotes and encourages independent reading, develops critical thinking skills, teaches the effective and ethical use of information sources, and promotes equitable access to all forms of information media.
- The mission of the School Library Program is to ensure that students and staff are effective users of resources, ideas, and information, and to promote the powers of literacy and competencies to function effectively as individuals and participate successfully in society.
- The mission of the _____ School Library Program is to ensure that students and staff are effective and efficient users of resources, ideas, and information literacy, and that they can evaluate information critically and competently.
- Through collaborative curriculum integration, the School Library Program empowers students to be critical thinkers, enthusiastic readers, skillful researchers, and ethical users of information.
- The School Library Program authentically engages students in developing twenty-first-century thinking skills; instructs them in the ethical use of technology and other sources while accessing, evaluating, and producing information; and prepares them to become lifelong readers.
- The mission of the School Library Program is to ensure that students and staff are effective users and producers of ideas and information, to promote literacy, and to develop students' competencies to be ethical participants in a global society.
- The _____ School District Library Program promotes and encourages independent reading, develops critical thinking skills, teaches the effective and ethical use of information sources, and promotes equitable access to all forms of information.

- The mission of the School Library Program is to promote lifelong learning, develop critical thinking skills in utilizing information resources, and acquire an appreciation of literature by providing opportunities for all students to gain the self-confidence necessary to successfully learn in an information-rich world.
- The Library Program provides and teaches effective and ethical uses of information, encourages critical thinking, promotes independent reading, offers readily and equitably accessible media sources to all users, and enhances personal and social responsibility.
- The School Library Program promotes the lifelong reading and learning habits needed to live in an increasingly complex global world by providing access to information, material, and instruction supporting the curriculum, state standards, and diverse learning needs of its students.
- In partnership with teachers, the School Library Program empowers students to be enthusiastic readers, critical thinkers, skillful researchers, and ethical users and producers of information in a global society.
- The School District Library Program promotes and encourages independent reading, develops critical thinking skills, teaches the effective and ethical use of information sources, and provides equitable access to all forms of information.
- The School Library Program takes students beyond textbooks to explore and solve questions requiring critical thinking and an understanding of the ethical uses of information so they become effective consumers and producers of ideas as well as lifelong readers.

Pick and Choose

Which three mission statements do you think are the best? Why?

1. _____

2. _____

3. _____

Which ones have weak words that can be strengthened?

What words or phrases from these statements do you think are most effective?

Review the statement you wrote and, based on your answers, rewrite it.

TAGLINES

Although your new working mission statement is now prominently displayed in your library, it takes more to firmly implant a continued awareness of the SLP in the minds of all stakeholders. The business world has learned the importance of branding, and many organizations have picked up on it. A brand is not just the name of a product but what the consumer associates with that product.

Branding statements are generally called *taglines*, and you have been subliminally absorbing them for years. The Home Depot reassures, "You can do it—We can help." Staples self-congratulates with "That was easy," and then sells a red Easy button and uses the word *easy* in various sales promotions. The *New York Times* has what might be one of the oldest brands: "All the news that's fit to print." The first part of that phrase highlights the company's perceived function of being the newspaper of record, while the second distances the newspaper from the tabloids.

The object of a tagline is to capture in a few words the essence of the product. Here are some examples:

- Allstate Insurance—You're in good hands
- American Express—Don't leave home without it
- Avis Rent A Car—We try harder
- Burger King—Have it your way
- Cadillac Escalade Hybrid—The future of luxury
- Campbell's Soup—M'm! M'm! Good!
- Folger's Coffee—The best part of wakin' up
- Ford—Drive one
- Geico Insurance Company—Fifteen minutes could save you 15% or more on your car insurance
- IHOP (International House of Pancakes)—Come hungry. Leave happy.
- KFC—Life tastes better with KFC
- Maxwell House Coffee—Good to the last drop
- McDonald's—I'm lovin' it
- Mt. Sinai Medical Center (New York)—Another day, another breakthrough
- Mountain Dew—Do the Dew
- Red Bull—Gives you wings
- Taco Bell—Think outside the bun
- UPS—What can Brown do for you?
- V8—Make every serving count
- Visiting Nurse Service of New York—We bring the caring home

- Volkswagon Beetle—Think small
- Volvo—For life
- Walmart—Save money. Live better.

Which of the slogans on the list were familiar to you? With some, you could even hum the accompanying jingle. Look at them again and ask yourself what message the company or organization was trying to convey. To what extent was it successful?

Taglines are changed frequently, although some become synonymous with the brand they identify. For the preceding list, you probably can recall some previous slogans. Think about why the company decided to go with a new one. Taglines used again and again in advertising become imprinted on the brains of listeners. By creating a tagline, you can do the same for the SLP. Think of the key message you want to send.

Some possibilities might be:

- Where every kid succeeds. (This is a variant on an AASL slogan.)
- Where the classroom meets the real world.
- Where learning never stops.
- Gateway to tomorrow.
- We go beyond our walls.
- Where reading becomes a way of life.

Once you have settled on a tagline, add it to everything that has the name of your school library on it. Your tagline belongs on your letterhead, the signature on your e-mail, your website, and your business cards. You want everyone to associate those words with your program.

If you launch a marketing program targeting a specific audience or project, create a new tagline that communicates this specific message. Be alert to new directions being taken by the administration. They may signal a need to redo your tagline.

Your Tag

Which of the suggested school library taglines best conveys what you want known about your program?

What other possible messages would you like to send?

Write two taglines and check them out with members of your target audience.

1. _____

2. _____

CORE VALUES

Condensing the purpose of the SLP to a brief mission statement and then writing a short message in a tagline means that you have left out a lot about who you are, why you are committed to what you do, and what deep-seated beliefs inform how you operate your program. Now you have a chance to express those ideas. *New on the Job: A School Library Media Specialist's Guide to Success* devoted much of the first chapter to describing how and why to write a philosophy statement.[6] For those of you who need such a statement for visits by an accrediting agency, this is the best approach, but others might prefer the easier-to-assimilate listing of core values. Even if you choose the narrative style of a philosophy statement, begin by identifying your values, as these will strengthen your statement.

A search on the phrase shows that many businesses find it important to highlight their core values. It is essential for you to do the same. Recognize that you are identifying your fundamental beliefs. These beliefs require no justification but help clarify what you stand for (and might fight for). They are the underpinnings of your program.

For example, Colgate lists caring, global teamwork, and continuous improvement as its core values, noting that these are part of everything the company does.[7] Each value is followed by an explanatory paragraph. Google has ten corporate values, including "Focus on the user and all else will follow" and "You can make money without doing evil."[8] Very brief descriptors are given for Google's values. Microsoft Australia lists six values with no comments, the first being "We act with integrity and honesty."[9] The nine Common Beliefs of AASL's *Standards for the 21st-Century Learner* basically are core values.[10] Read them over, including the descriptive paragraphs. You may find that AASL has said it all for you. On the other hand, you may have other values that are equally important to you. For example, you might want one on respect, explaining that students and staff are entitled to be treated with courtesy and respect at all times.

Check your district or school website. Are core values posted? If they are, which of them do you want to include on your list? Do you feel these values are really being incorporated into daily practice? As you develop your own list, keep the total down. Twenty or more would be too much to handle on a daily basis.

Finding Your Core

1. Which of the AASL core values fit best with who you are and what you want your program to present to the world?

2. What other core values do you hold?

3. List at least four core values and then write a brief explanation of each.

_____

_____

_____

YOUR ELEVATOR TALK

In the business world, job hunters as well as those seeking to expand their customer base know they need to have an "elevator talk." You never know whom you might meet, and you must be prepared to pitch your product—in this case, the SLP. You can write your own elevator talk or make it the topic of a district school librarians' meeting, but make sure you have one ready.

The chief feature of an elevator talk is its brevity. It should be under a minute, or about the time it takes a high-speed elevator to get passengers up or down several floors. The best elevator talks have four parts:

- bold opening statement
- explanation
- statistic
- invitation

For example, your opening might be "No one in the entire school system can replace the instruction given by the school librarian." That is definitely an attention-getter. Follow it up with a *brief* explanation (you are working with a tight time limit) of what makes your school library unique and why that feature is so valuable.

You have a wealth of research to draw on to find your statistics. Choose from the ones included in *School Libraries Work!* issued by Scholastic Library Publishing.[11] It is available as a pdf download, or you can contact the publisher for copies.

If appropriate, close your talk with an invitation to see the SLP in action. If this is not feasible, suggest that your listener can learn more at the AASL website, www.aasl.org. To learn more about the role played by all types of libraries, listeners can go to www.ilovelibraries.org, a site created by ALA.

Once you have written your elevator talk, commit it to memory. You have to have it down cold so that it comes out naturally whenever you need it. As you practice, listen for any "bumps" that keep it from flowing smoothly, and make the necessary corrections.

Who gets to hear your elevator talk? Just about anyone. Trot it out when you are in line at the supermarket if the conversation turns the right way (or guide it there). Use it with your parent volunteers or even teachers. Your talk should not minimize their value in any way, so it should not upset them. If someone comes to pick up equipment for repair and comments on how different your facility looks compared to school libraries of twenty years ago, respond with your talk.

As with your mission statement and tagline, your elevator talk keeps you and your program highly visible to just about every stakeholder with whom you come in contact. Each stakeholder has a separate function. Know your target audiences for all functions. Although these may overlap, the situation will define which message you send.

Canned Talk

1. Write the "bold statement" you will use to open your elevator talk.

   _____

2. List two sentences that will explain your opening.

   _____

   _____

3. Who will be your best audience for this?
4. When can you see yourself using an elevator talk?

KEY IDEAS

- To be seen as indispensable you must continually prove that you and the SLP are essential for achieving the school's mission and goals.
- You must become a building leader.
- Develop and hone your advocacy skills.
- Identify the aspects of the educational program that are your responsibility, requiring your unique expertise.
- A mission statement proclaims the purpose and importance of the SLP.
- A tagline is a brand that conveys the essence of your role.
- Core values, like a philosophy, encapsulate your fundamental beliefs about the SLP.
- Include an elevator talk in your repertoire. Write one, memorize it, and be prepared to use it.

Notes

1. American Association of School Librarians (AASL), *Standards for the 21st-Century Learner* (Chicago: American Library Association, 2007), 2.
2. American Association of School Librarians (AASL), *Empowering Learners: Guidelines for School Library Media Programs* (Chicago: American Association of School Librarians, 2009).
3. Educational Testing Service, www.ets.org.
4. The Partnership for 21st Century Skills, www.p21.org. Retrieved March 27, 2009.

5. American Association of School Librarians (AASL), Association for Educational Communications and Technology, *Information Power: Building Partnerships for Learning* (Chicago: American Library Association, 1998).

6. R. Toor and H. K. Weisburg, *New on the Job: A School Library Media Specialist's Guide to Success* (Chicago: American Library Association, 2007), 2–11.

7. Colgate World of Care, "Colgate's Core Values," www.colgate.com/app/Colgate/US/Corp/LivingOurValues/CoreValues.cvsp.

8. Google, "Google Corporate Values," http://googlesystem.blogspot.com/2005/10/google-corporate-values.html.

9. Microsoft Corporation, "Our Mission and Core Values," www.microsoft.com/australia/citizenship/about/mission.mspx.

10. AASL, *Standards for the 21st-Century Learner,* 2–3.

11. Scholastic Library Publishing, *School Libraries Work!,* 3rd ed. (2008), www2.scholastic.com/content/collateral_resources/pdf/s/slw3_2008.pdf.

CHAPTER 2
What Makes a Leader?

Follow me. It's going to be fun and exciting!

With your mission, tagline, and core values in place—at least in the rough draft stage—it is time to focus on what you need to do and how you need to be in order to become a leader, indispensable to your school and district. Before addressing that issue, however, you must first rid yourself of some misconceptions.

AUTHORITY VERSUS LEADERSHIP

When asked to name district and building leaders, most people's usual first response is to list the superintendent of schools, principals, supervisors, and coordinators. This list might be accurate in a narrow sense, but it is far too limiting. Although these people hold positions of authority with the right to reward or punish, they are not necessarily leaders, and having the ability to compel others to follow directives is not *leadership*.

Anyone who has been in the job market for a number of years, in education or any other field, has dealt with titles granting authority to people who are totally lacking in leadership skills. In dealing with administrators who fall into this category, staff members tend to find work-around solutions to get things done.

Instead of naming someone with a title, think about the go-to individuals who make things work in your school or district. Sometimes it is a super-efficient secretary, but it can be anyone who understands how to get things done and knows the appropriate direction in which to go. You can probably name two or three people in your building who fall into this category.

In order for you to be a leader, people must follow you. The staff will do only what they absolutely must for authority figures with little or no leadership abilities. Remember the childhood game Follow the Leader? Some kids were a natural. They knew how to make the game fun. The risks were minimal but exciting. Other kids were boring, and the game quickly broke up. Some were thoughtlessly daring, and you quickly learned that disasters ensued when they led. The same positive and negative traits are present in adults. Although it is no longer a game, you instinctively know whom to follow and whom to avoid.

The point is that you do not need a title to become a building leader. When you exhibit the skills and attributes of leadership, people begin to follow you. For some, this result comes naturally. Others must consciously choose to take on this responsibility. As a school librarian who wants to become indispensable, you have no other choice.

Authority Figures and Leaders

1. What are two characteristics of administrators who are not leaders?

   _____

   _____

2. What strategies have you observed teachers and staff using to deal with the lack of leadership at the top?

3. Identify at least one building leader who is not an administrator.

4. Why did you choose this person?

QUALITIES OF A LEADER

When you explained the reasons why you named the staff person as a building leader, you were recognizing important qualities. Although people may identify a variety of attributes, certain ones invariably appear on everyone's list. These include professional as well as personal characteristics. Most notably, leaders have a vision. In addition, they must be articulate and persuasive. There is no sense in following someone who does not have any idea where to go. At the same time, leaders must be able to express their ideas in a way that resonates with others and makes them *want* to help achieve the goal.

Along with these qualities, leaders must be willing to take risks and accept responsibility for failure. They shoulder any blame, but share success broadly. There is a strong sense of participating in something worthwhile. Underlying all these attributes is competence. Leaders know their stuff; they have done their homework and can see the bigger picture.

On a personal level, the most important quality of a leader is trustworthiness. Leaders have integrity and principles. You can count on their word. In addition, good leaders are persistent and diligent. Most of all, they have a sense of humor. They take what they do seriously and themselves lightly. They know laughter helps everyone through the roughest times.

Creating a catalog of leadership qualities is a first step. Learning how these qualities translate into the workplace takes additional effort. In the next sections of this chapter, you will have an opportunity to become more familiar with these traits and see how to incorporate them into your own style. As you master them, you will become a building leader—the person whom others count on; the one they go to with a question or problem; a key player when decisions are made.

Quality Leadership

1. Think of the best administrator you have had. Which of the traits mentioned did he or she possess?

2. Were any traits missing?

3. Think of the worst administrator you have had. How many of the traits mentioned did he or she possess?

4. Which traits were most notably missing?

CREATING A VISION

As previously noted, the first leadership quality everyone identifies is vision. The corollary is this: if you do not have a vision, you cannot be a leader. You write one, frequently with help from others, not as a personal statement but as what you envision for the SLP. Although many confuse a vision statement with the mission, there are distinct differences.

Mission defines *purpose*, while vision, as stated in *New on the Job,*[1] is about how you wish to be perceived and what you would achieve in an ideal world. Though your mission statement was about what you *are*, your vision is directed toward what you want to *become*. It resembles the Big Audacious Goal created as part of a strategic plan. Seeing it written down should make you gasp. Your head should be chanting, "This will never happen." If your vision is big enough, probably your head is correct. But that is not the point. You have just set the direction in which you want to go and identified the road to this distant place of near-perfection.

From this point forward, your actions, in addition to being aligned with your mission and core values, should be leading your program toward this ultimate goal. However, recall that in order to lead you must have followers—otherwise you are walking alone. Thoreau might champion a majority of one and hear a different drummer; you, on the other hand, need all the partners you can get. Rather than Thoreau, take Emerson and his "hitch your wagon to a star" as a guide. Although you might not achieve your vision, if you aim very high you will accomplish far more than you dreamed possible.

Your vision must be inspiring and compelling. Just thinking about the possibility of making it happen should give you energy to go forward on days when details threaten to drag you down. Others in the educational community should find it equally exciting. If your vision is ever to be realized, your colleagues and your administrators must see the value and importance of being part of that journey.

In creating your vision, consider what the SLP could be if money and staff were not an issue. Thing big and think futuristically. Envision the library ten or more years down the road. This is a no-holds-barred exercise. Do not let yourself be fettered by the practical or concerns about the doable. You want it *all*. *But* you must be sure that what you want is what administrators, teachers, students, parents, and local business leaders will recognize as being invaluable to their own aspirations and needs.

Write your vision in the present tense, as though it were a current reality. Although not everyone does this, having it in the present keeps you from thinking your envisioned world exists only in a distant tomorrow. Every plan you make should be leading you there, so keep it as inspiration in your daily life.

Corporations and organizations that have created visions feature them as frequently as they do their mission statements. AASL posts its vision statement on its web page.

The American Association of School Librarians is:

- A proactive organization that addresses issues, anticipates trends, and sets the future agenda for the profession;
- An advocate for the indispensable role of school library media programs with school library media specialists, for best practices in school librarianship, and for the core values and ethics of the library profession;
- An open, friendly, welcoming organization that embraces cultural and ethnic diversity;
- An inclusive professional home for all school library media specialists and a partner in mutual interests with educators, technologists, researchers, vendors, and other librarians;
- An essential resource for school library media specialists seeking professional development, leadership opportunities, communication with peers, and the most current information, research, and theory in the field; and
- A flexible, responsive organization that models effective management practices.

(Adopted by the AASL Board of Directors, January 2003)[2]

You can see that some items in the AASL statement are currently true, while other points are distinctly part of a desired future. However, everything is written in the present tense.

Differing views exist about the length of a vision statement. Although most people agree that mission statements should be brief, some believe visions can be longer. AASL's statement falls into the latter category. When writing yours, try for a shorter version. For one thing, it is easier to remember and quote when you are not in your library. For another, a short statement can be framed and hung just as you did with your mission.

Envisioning the SLP

1. Picture your SLP as though you were describing the perfect program.
2. What would the environment be like?
3. Who would be served and how?
4. What great outcomes would be achieved? (Think students here.)
5. List at least five phrases that describe your answers.

_____

_____

_____

_____

_____

6. Wordsmith your phrases into a draft vision statement.

_____

Sample Visions

As with the mission statement in chapter 1, now that you have given your vision some thought, you can look more objectively at ones that others have written. The following samples were created by workshop participants working against a time clock and by graduate students still learning about SLPs. They should be considered drafts. Look for nuggets of good ideas as well as words and phrases that are inspiring. Compare them with what you envisioned.

- The students of the _____ School District achieve through continuing access, self-checkout, and information literacy, in a welcoming environment, and in accordance with state standards.
- The _____ Library Program is the heartbeat of the whole community, nurturing in our students a love for reading and the desire to learn, preparing them for the rest of their lives.
- The Library Program is the heart of the school where, in partnership with teachers, students are nurtured to grow and develop a love of reading, deeper understandings of the world of information, and an appreciation of their own talents and interests, paving the way to a successful future.

- The School Library Program is the hub of our community of learners, engendering a love for reading and expanding students' and teachers' abilities to be active participants in the global interchange of information.
- The School Library Program is the access point for students and teachers, enabling them to use current print and technology resources to pursue academic and personal interests.
- The School Library Program is the heart of the educational community. Love of the written word and the research skills for intellectual and personal achievement are grown and nurtured here.
- The School Library Program is a learner-centered environment where up-to-date resources and technology and a responsive staff empower students and teachers to achieve their academic and personal goals.
- The School Library acts as a dynamic agent of learning that fosters the development of lifelong learners who are effective users of ideas and information acquired through a variety of sources and technologies.
- The School Library provides a place for individuals of all abilities, genders, races, and creeds to find a welcome in their search for knowledge, whether formal or informal, in an environment that fosters cooperation and collaboration and an attitude of excitement toward the learning process.
- The _____ School Library Program prepares students to meet the challenges of the future creating meaningful and diverse learning opportunities for all students so they can develop the skills necessary to succeed.
- The school library program provides resources and learning activities that represent a diversity of experiences, opinions, and social and cultural perspectives.
- Students of the _____ School Library Program are empowered with creative and authentic learning opportunities and experiences that prepare them for success in the twenty-first century.
- The vision of the _____ library program is to instill lifelong learning skills in students, guiding them to become fluent in technology and manage the world of information to benefit from the free flow of ideas in ever-changing formats.
- The school library program is a collaborative and instructional partnership between students, teachers, school librarians,

administrators, and the community, preparing students to be
successful in an unknowable future.

- The school librarian is part of the everyday instructional fabric of
the school, supporting instruction, research, lifelong appreciation
for humanities and preparing students for the twenty-first-century
workplace by creating a multicultural, relevant and unbiased,
supportive learning environment complete with twenty-first-
century tools.

- The vision of the school library program is that all students and
staff enjoy an ongoing exchange of information and learning that
ensures their success in the twenty-first century.

- The _____ Library is a virtual part of every classroom, recognized
as essential by the entire educational community for increasing
student achievement and readiness to participate in the global society.

- The _____ Library Program is a key contributor to the
district's goals of developing world-class students able to compete
successfully and take their place in the digital community of the
twenty-first century.

Pick and Choose—Again

1. Which three visions do you think are the best? Why?

   _____

   _____

   _____

2. Which ones have weak words that can be strengthened?
3. What words or phrases from these statements do you think are most effective?
4. Review the statement you wrote and, based on your answers, rewrite it.

PROFESSIONAL SKILLS OF A LEADER

By creating a vision you have taken the first step to leadership. Now it is time to
look more closely at other attributes to find out to what extent you have them
and how they can be increased and honed. If you want to get your message
out, you must be articulate and persuasive. Honestly assess your communication
skills. Although having the ability to write well is helpful in preparing reports
and memos (hard copy or e-mail), your daily conversations and discussions will
make the greatest impact overall.

Speaking well is not always the same as speaking to the point. Particularly when dealing with administrators, you need to focus on your target message. Stakeholders do not have time for you to overwhelm them with detail. If you think it necessary, just inform them that you can provide the additional information when needed. Knowing your mission, vision, and philosophy will keep your words on track. As any politician can tell you, it is critical to "stay on message."

To polish your skills in this area, become active in professional associations. Being a member is a basic step, but you must participate to derive the true benefits. If you have not volunteered for your state library organization, do so now. If you already are doing that, go national. AASL has virtual committee members, so the inability to travel to conferences is no longer a barrier. Leaders must be knowledgeable and have a grasp of the larger issues. Understanding the needs of your SLP is not sufficient. Becoming active in these associations widens your access to experts in school librarianship and exposes you to discussions about trends in education. Active participation further builds your fluency in discussing important concerns. Your awareness of these issues increases, as does the vocabulary that makes you sound like the authority you are becoming. Your convincing language and understanding of what is happening in the larger world convey competence, and people are then willing to follow you.

Always remember as you are presenting your message that it does not matter how important you know it is. The message must connect to something of significance to the listener, or you will not get the support you want. Many school librarians have talked within their buildings about research studies and other data, but too often they sound as though the information had value only to the SLP. The bigger connection had not been made strongly enough.

Willingness to take a risk and willingness to accept responsibility for failure are two qualities that freeze school librarians and keep them from becoming leaders. Charting a new course always involves the possibility that it will not work as anticipated. Yet, if you do not propose a new direction and instead embrace the status quo, you are not leading. Keep in mind that a failure is not failing. You fail only when you quit.

Just as you do not want your students to be afraid of making mistakes, you should not be fearful either. They and you must recognize the good things as well. Having something go wrong is an opportunity for learning. Honestly acknowledge where your proposal did not work, and then go forward.

Minimize potential setbacks by behaving as though you are not the only one who knows what to do. Instead, encourage those working with you to communicate their concerns and misgivings. This feedback helps reveal problems before they have a chance to become so large you cannot redirect your efforts. Being able to change course requires flexibility, another hallmark of leadership.

Fortunately, this quality is the one that most school librarians have already had to develop in order to manage daily routines.

Professional Attributes

1. Which of the qualities discussed do you consider your strongest?
2. Which is the one you feel is your weakest quality?
3. What is your plan for strengthening it?

PERSONAL CHARACTERISTICS OF A LEADER

Although expertise and the other qualities just mentioned are important to your being recognized as a leader, the most valuable attribute is integrity. You must be trustworthy, or people will not follow you. Trusting your judgment and knowledge is only one aspect. People need to know you will not turn on them or violate their confidences.

As you work with staff and possibly administrators, they will often express opinions or reveal personal issues. Even if they do not expressly ask you to keep such information confidential, you must be careful not to repeat what you are told. School systems run on gossip. You must *never* be a party to it. You will most likely slip up on occasion. But if you are mindful of the potential for harm, you will probably repeat only what is in general circulation rather than regale others with something told only to you.

Persistence is another attribute to cultivate. Smart administrators have learned that if they refuse initial requests or do not respond to proposals raised by faculty members, most of these will go away. This tactic prevents their plates from being loaded by those who initiate ideas but have no follow-through. Any time or money given to someone who does not know how to get a job done, no matter how good the concept, will be wasted because the project will inevitably fail. Administrators do not want to get involved unless there is some assurance of success.

If you are turned down the first time, do not consider the decision final. Creativity comes into play here, because you cannot go back to an administrator or supervisor with the same idea you brought initially. Look at your proposal. What other slant could you take? Are there important benefits you did not include? Listen carefully to any reasons you were given for the rejection. Talk it over with those who thought you were on the right track. Then rethink, reword, and resubmit. Keep at it. You may have to do this more than once or twice, but eventually your idea will be heard. Perseverance is frequently rewarded, but it must be accompanied by diligence. Good leaders work harder than anyone else.

On the other hand, do not try to do everything yourself. Learn to delegate, giving partners ownership in the outcome. They become empowered through their efforts and derive personal and professional satisfaction from working with you. Although others are managing different aspects of the project, stay current with the status of all its parts. You should know who is doing what and be ready to assist those experiencing difficulties with their piece. If you demonstrate that mistakes or dropped details do not cause you to blame the person but rather are an indication that you failed to foresee where she or he might need assistance, people will come to you as soon as they are in trouble. Remember to inspire, inspect, and then inspire again.

One leadership attribute that will keep you from jumping all over someone who has made an error is empathy. Recognize that the person feels guilty and embarrassed. No one wants to get it wrong. Although you cannot pretend that the problem did not occur, you can discuss the best approach for fixing it. Also explore what can be done to avoid such snafus in the future. By taking setbacks in stride while looking for alternatives to move forward, you put a positive spin on the situation and will undoubtedly gain increased loyalty and support from the one who caused the difficulty.

Accept the fact that not everyone will agree with you. Even those supportive and part of your plan may at times think you are making a mistake. How you handle criticism will affect your success as a leader. Never become defensive. Active listening is imperative. Although coming up with rebuttal statements is natural, you must suppress that impulse. Focus on what is being said. Restate it, asking whether you understood the comments correctly. Encourage the person to make a suggestion that would take care of the perceived problem. Knowing they are being heard makes people feel their opinions are important, and you might be surprised to realize they have a point.

Regularly take stock of why you are pursuing this course of action. When colleagues begin looking to you for advice and leadership, it can quickly become an ego trip. Once your ego is engaged, those positive professional and personal qualities get lost in self-congratulatory behaviors. Focus on the outcomes to be achieved rather than glorying at being center stage.

Another trait of great leaders is passion. They love what they do and feel strongly about their commitments. Sometimes this enthusiasm seems like charisma, but it is born from their enthusiasm for what they are doing. This exuberance, when coupled with the other attributes already discussed, is contagious. Everyone loves being with people who are passionate and so are inclined to follow in the direction they lead.

Last, but certainly not least, is the need for leaders to have a sense of humor. You cannot survive if you take yourself too seriously. Be ready to laugh at yourself even while you promote the importance of what you are trying to achieve.

Additionally, laugh at the absurdities that are an inevitable aspect of any bureau-cracy such as a public school system. This does not mean making sarcastic jokes about the "idiocy" of the administration or whatever barrier you are facing. Simply accept that this is how things sometimes are. If you see it as funny rather than as a threat, your humor will ease any tensions. Draw on your ability to be flexible. Whatever the problem, you can usually find the means to work around it.

Personal Characteristics

1. Which of the qualities discussed do you consider your strongest?
2. Which is the one you feel is your weakest quality?
3. What is your plan for strengthening it?

NETS AS A LEAD-IN TO LEADERSHIP

National and state standards have become an established aspect of education. In working with teachers, you address their professional standards, but two other sets of standards are also part of your domain. The first set is the National Educational Technology Standards (NETS) from the International Society for Technology in Education (ISTE). Because the ISTE membership includes tech-nology teachers and directors, classroom teachers, and school librarians, what it produces is automatically a collaborative effort.

In 1998, ISTE published NETS for Students (NETS-S), Teachers (NETS-T), and Administrators (NETS-A) to further its mission of providing "leadership and service to improve teaching and learning by advancing the effective use of tech-nology in education."[3] In 2007, it refreshed NETS-S. The following year it did the same for NETS-T, and then continued with NETS-A. Although these easily accepted standards focus solely on integrating technology into education, you can use them as a means to establish your leadership in this area.

You begin with these standards because everyone wants students to be highly proficient in using technology. The fact that project sponsors include Adobe, Apple, Intel, and Microsoft adds to the standards' credibility with administra-tors and teachers. Discussing the six NETS-S standards with your principal dem-onstrates your awareness of an identified target that should be addressed.

NETS-T mirrors NETS-S. For example, the first standard for students pro-motes "Creativity and Innovation," while teachers are expected to "Facilitate and Inspire Student Learning and Creativity."[4] (NETS-A expects administrators to provide the leadership and create the environment that promotes the achieve-ment of the standards.) One of your unique skills is knowing how to integrate technology into classroom units. By offering to give workshops to teachers, you establish yourself as someone who recognizes the direction in which education is going and has the ability to help others get there.

Incorporating phraseology from NETS into your conversations with teachers, administrators, and parents makes you sound knowledgeable about an important focus of education. When you use such terms as *information fluency*, *decision-making skills*, and *digital citizenship*, others want to know more. They realize the importance of what you are saying and see the need to develop their own understanding in this area. In turning to you for information, they recognize you as a leader.

You can download the one-page list of standards for free from the NETS website, www.iste.org/nets, but you should purchase the twenty-five-page hard copy, which gives additional information. NETS-S has scenarios from all over the world, with different grade levels and subject areas and with profiles presenting brief examples of what students should be doing in grades PK–2, 3–5, 6–8, and 9–12. NETS-T includes rubrics and scenarios for each of the standards. Offer to purchase *Making Technology Standards Work for You* (2nd ed.) by Susan J. Brooks-Young for your principal from the ISTE bookstore, and do a quick read while cataloging it.

Although when introducing NETS your focus is on classroom teachers and administrators, make a point of involving the computer teacher and informing the technology department of what you are doing and purchasing. The interweaving of technology into the curriculum is your unique role, but these two stakeholders have a piece of that pie. You want to make them partners, not adversaries. Remember, claiming your territory is different from being territorial. You will not succeed if others view you as seizing the glory or ignoring their expertise.

NETS Assets

1. Which of the NETS-S standards do you think is most challenging for your students?
2. Which standard do you think is easiest for them?
3. Which of the NETS-T standards do you think is most challenging for teachers?
4. Which standard do you think is easiest for them?
5. Which NETS-T standard would make the best lead-in to get your teachers thinking about what you can offer them?

SOLIDIFYING YOUR POSITION WITH THE AASL STANDARDS

Once administrators and teachers have benefited from your introduction of NETS, you are ready to move to the next level. Although NETS establishes your credibility in knowing the technology students must master, AASL's *Standards for the 21st-Century Learner* give you the resources to ensure that students are truly prepared for their future. You can get the standards as a free download, but, as a leader, it is far wiser to purchase a pack of twelve and distribute copies as needed. Like NETS, these standards incorporate technology, but they go beyond those competencies to focus on how learners must "use skills, resources, and tools" to be successful in the digital world.[5]

The simplicity of four standards, each building on the previous one, makes it easy for you to highlight your contribution as an instructional partner and teacher. Your administrators will appreciate how farseeing these standards are, because they are not limited to skills. Each standard has four strands: (1) the familiar *Skills*, but also (2) Dispositions in Action, which addresses whether students are developing the intellectual behaviors needed to "gain and share knowledge," (3) *Responsibilities*, which focuses heavily on behaviors and traits that recognize the importance of participating with others, and (4) *Self-Assessment Strategies* for monitoring learning to be sure that practices are effective.[6]

A number of school librarians were concerned about the word *disposition* in the standards, but the term is quite familiar to supervisors and administrators, who will be impressed that you are incorporating it into your teaching. Because administrators and supervisors are so well acquainted with the concept, you should take time to understand it yourself *before* discussing it with them. Look at the indicators for Dispositions in Action and see what is required. Most likely, these goals will make sense to you, but quite possibly you have not yet incorporated them into your teaching.

Obviously you will need to make adjustments. Begin with a unit or lesson that you have presented. Was it inquiry-based? The Skills strand requires that. If it was not, think of how you can revise it. Once you have done so, you can work your way through the other three strands. However, in order to incorporate the new standards into your teaching you probably will need to revise your curriculum. Meet with your colleagues in the district and present a plan for revision to the administration. The request is a demonstration of your being a leader. The resulting curriculum should reinforce that recognition.

Two other resources are critical in helping you establish the AASL *Standards for the 21st-Century Learner* in your program by interweaving them throughout the other subject curricula. *Standards for the 21st-Century Learner in Action*[7] is essential for writing that new curriculum, giving you benchmarks, assessments, scenarios, and examples of lessons. *Empowering Learners: Guidelines for School Library Media Programs*[8] supersedes *Information Power: Building Partnerships for Learning*. It provides guidelines and actions for: "Teaching for Learning," "Building the Learning Environment," and "Empowering Learning through

Leadership." You might also want to download *Learning4Life*,[9] the national implementation plan for the new standards that offers ideas for bringing them to your district and school.

As an educational leader, you must have a solid grasp of your area of expertise. You must be familiar and comfortable with the new standards and guidelines. Before working on a revised curriculum, look for workshops in your state to help you work through these publications and develop confidence in using them. The new terminology will soon be part of your vocabulary.

Twenty-First-Century Standards

1. What is the importance of using the term *learners* rather than *students* in the new standards?

2. Which of the four strands do you find easiest to address?

3. Which one is most challenging for you?

4. Which classroom/subject units would benefit most from incorporating these standards with your help?

KEY IDEAS

- Being a leader does not require a title of authority.
- Leaders must have an inspiring vision that others will want to see realized.
- Leaders possess the following qualities and skills:
  Strong communication skills (articulate and persuasive)
  Willingness to take risks and accept responsibility for mistakes
  Readiness to share success widely
  Expertise in their field
  Ability to see the big picture
- Personal attributes of leaders include:
  Trustworthiness
  Persistence
  Diligence
  Empathy
  Creativity
  Flexibility
  Passion
  Sense of humor

- Familiarity with national standards establishes your credibility as a leader.
- NETS, because they deal exclusively with technology and are cross-curricular, provide an excellent way to initiate new directions.
- The American Association of School Librarians' *Standards for the 21st-Century Learner*, addressing the skills and behaviors necessary for student success in a digital world, is aligned with current trends in education.

Notes

1. R. Toor and H. K. Weisburg, *New on the Job: A School Library Media Specialist's Guide to Success* (Chicago: American Library Association, 2007), 2.
2. American Association of School Librarians, "AASL Vision Statement," www.ala.org/ala/mgrps/divs/aasl/aboutaasl/aaslvision/aaslvisionstatement.cfm.
3. International Society for Technology in Education, "About ISTE," www.iste.org.
4. International Society for Technology in Education, "National Educational Technology Standards," www.iste.org/nets.
5. American Association of School Librarians, *Standards for the 21st-Century Learner* (Chicago: American Library Association, 2007), 3.
6. Ibid., 3–8.
7. American Association of School Librarians, *Standards for the 21st-Century Learner in Action* (Chicago: AASL, 2009).
8. American Association of School Librarians, *Empowering Learners: Guidelines for School Library Media Programs* (Chicago: AASL, 2009).
9. *Learning4Life*, www.ala.org/ala/mgrps/divs/aasl/guidelinesandstandards/learning4life/document/download.cfm.

CHAPTER 3
Where Do You Stand?

Just where do I belong? How do I fit everything in so that I stand out?

When you have a title that conveys a leadership role, such as *principal*, most of your time is spent in leading. (Although, as noted in chapter 2, not everyone is successful at it.) Becoming an indispensable building leader without an official position is not nearly that simple. You must establish yourself by actions and ideas without any appearance of trying to exert your will over others.

Oddly, your accomplishments can create new problems. There will be those who think you have some magic and will try to enlist you in myriad projects that have no connection to your mission or vision. A few, resenting anyone who is successful, may attempt to thwart your plans. Meanwhile, you have many other jobs that must be done. How do you stay on track and not lose your cool?

Good leaders are keenly aware of the environment and culture in which they operate. In addition, they not only "don't sweat the small stuff," they do not appear to sweat at all. If you seem frazzled and harried, people lose confidence in you. Think of yourself as a swan swimming effortlessly across a lake while underneath you are paddling like mad.

ASSESSING YOURSELF

You are about to embark on a concerted plan to ensure that you are seen as indispensable. In the business world, no one would consider launching a significant campaign without first doing an environmental scan. *You* should do one as well. Throughout this process you must be scrupulously honest. Neither sugarcoat reality nor make it worse than it is.

What you are looking at are your strengths and weaknesses. No one is great in all areas, but everyone has places where they excel. For example, are you uncomfortable talking in front of large groups? A great number of people are. This discomfort would affect your approach to the business community. Obviously, you would not speak at a Rotary meeting as your initial overture. Are you a resident with strong local contacts outside school? These connections keep you aware of major concerns that you can address from the library perspective.

Spend some time creating your list. You cannot set aside an hour and just get it done. Plan on taking a week during which you will observe yourself in action. What do you do that seems to spark a connection with others? Where do they take a step back from you? Do you hear yourself talking more than listening?

The job of a school librarian is multifaceted. Despite all your expertise in the field, you do some things better than others. Where do you stand out? To what extent is that special skill worthwhile to those in your building or district? Do you have skills that are technically not part of your job but would be regarded as valuable within the school setting? You might be able to coach or to play the piano for a performance. One school librarian decided her middle school needed a literary magazine, so she created one. You need to look at your abilities to find where you can weave your way into the fabric of the educational community.

Test your self-assessment with others. Check with friends in and out of the building. Let them know you are trying to become better at what you do and, therefore, need to know what you have to work with—and against. If you encourage them to respond honestly, you might be upset with some of their comments. Do not let your distress show. Thank them; you will want their help later. Accept what they say as being at least possibly, if not probably, true.

Strengths and Weaknesses

1. Which single strength of yours were you surprised to discover?

2. What weakness is causing you concern?

3. Do you think it can be moderated?

4. What is your strongest asset?

CHECKING YOUR SURROUNDINGS

Having conducted an internal scan, you now move to an external one. Typically this means looking for opportunities and threats, but that sounds overly dramatic for a personal survey. Instead, you are looking for where you have made good alliances (future opportunities) or have in some way alienated various people.

Begin your scan by assessing how you and your program are perceived. In making your determination, recognize that actions mean far more than words. Everyone has heard principals say, "The library is the heart of our school," and then cut the budget, take away library space, or give extraneous duties to the school librarian. Lip service to the SLP is not worth anything.

Make a list of key people in your building. This includes star teachers and those known as troublemakers. Custodians, secretaries, and volunteers also belong on the list, as do students. Consider how they interact with you, your facility, and your program. Are they holding these in high regard, valuing the contribution you make? Try asking the ones you get along with best how *they* view what you do. Prepare yourself not to engage in a debate should their comments be more negative than you feel is justified. You need to know where you stand. Are you a priority with anyone? Be as honest with yourself as possible.

On a piece of paper, create three columns. In the first, put all the people with whom you have a strong, positive relationship. In the middle one, record those who are neutral about you. In the last column, place any who dislike you or impede your actions or both. (A number of you might have the tech department in this last category.)

If you have been good at your job, there should be almost no one in the third column. Most people with whom you interact will be in the second. The more you have in the first one, the better shape you are in.

Now analyze who is where. Are any major players among those who put barriers in your way? Perhaps you experience difficulties with the aforementioned tech department or the principal. Who are your supporters? Are they high-profile teachers, the quiet ones, or the rabble-rousers? Do you have any board of education members in the first group? Is the PTA president a volunteer in your library and an ally? How do the majority of students feel about you? Do they consider you an important resource and vital helper, or are you just another adult in their lives? If you are going to succeed as a leader and be regarded as indispensable, you need a significant number of the key people believing that what you do is *invaluable* to the school community.

Friends and Foes

1. Which group or person constitutes your greatest support?
2. Does this group or person have power over your potential success?
3. Are there any powerful persons or groups in the negative camp?
4. How are teachers split among the three categories?

PERSONAL STRATEGIC PLANNING

Organizations and businesses do strategic planning to ensure that their efforts are focused toward achieving desired outcomes. The process takes a long time, is usually led by a facilitator, and frequently involves focus groups. The result is a document that outlines the organization's direction for the next three to five years. It identifies several big goals, yearly action steps, the person or group responsible for each one, dates when these are to be accomplished, and, sometimes, an assessment to evaluate results. The plan is revisited annually and tweaked as necessary.

College graduates, particularly those going into business careers, are often encouraged to create three-to-five-year plans for their future. Although they may not achieve everything they set out to do, they are far more likely to get close to their targets than are those who just let life happen to them. Even in a good job market, personal strategic planning is a sensible approach to keeping your life in balance and reducing wasted efforts.

Without realizing it, you have already begun working on your strategic plan. You have identified your core values and conducted an internal and external scan of your environment. What you need next is a Big Audacious Goal (BAG) that powers you forward. Usually, this takes some time to create because you want to reach really high. However, for the purpose of this book, your BAG is obvious. You want to weave yourself so completely into the fabric of the educational community that it would be impossible to remove you without causing drastic holes. If you think that goal is unattainable, you have identified your BAG. Everything you do should get you closer to realizing it.

Because the mission and vision statements you created for your program will work for your personal strategic plan, you can move forward to the next phase. Set three or four large goals. You might decide, for example, to "develop personal relationships with teachers" or "participate in extracurricular programs." None of these goals should necessarily be achievable in a single year.

Next, outline doable action steps for the current school year. For example, if you are working toward the goal of developing relationships with teachers, your action plan could be to "learn what mutual hobbies and interests I share with at least five teachers." Committing to attending plays and other evening programs during the school year or sponsoring a club could be action steps for the second goal of participating in extracurricular programs.

The sample page for your personal strategic plan (figure 1) shows how you might work on one goal during a single school year. You can have one action step or several. However, you do not want to overburden yourself. Particularly in the first year, keep it simple. Choose steps that clearly get you to your desired goal. Achieving success with even one goal will help power you to go further the following year.

FIGURE 1
SAMPLE PAGE FOR PERSONAL STRATEGIC PLAN

GOAL: To develop personal relationships with teachers

Action Step	With Whom	Details	Completed By	Evaluation
Engage in a personal conversation with at least one teacher per week	Teachers who frequent the school library	Ask to help them and inquire about their interests	End of school year	At least 5 teachers and I share some common interest that we discuss with each other.

Put your personal strategic plan on a spreadsheet or create a table in word processing. Keep track of the due dates you set. The purpose of the plan is to keep you focused on achieving your goals. You will not get them if you duck deadlines. This does not mean that you will not have to make adjustments. You might have thought you made a connection, but the teacher became too busy, or not enough teachers seem to stay in the school library long enough to strike up a conversation.

One more thought about your strategic plan. This is a personal plan, just for you, and you have a life outside your job. It is very easy to get caught up in the tasks and demands of the day and neglect the important priorities of family and friends. Make sure you have one goal relating to enjoying time with those who mean the most to you. Having to put them into a plan may seem as though you are taking away the spontaneity of these relationships, but that is better than overlooking them and feeling overworked, overwhelmed, and underappreciated as a result.

At this point, it should be obvious that you are not going to achieve your BAG in the immediate future. What you are striving to do takes time. Even so, at the end of the first year, if you worked on action plans for each of your goals, you will see signs that you are becoming increasingly important to several of the constituencies you are trying to reach. Each succeeding year will bring you ever closer.

My Personal Plan

1. What three or four goals have you set for your personal strategic plan?

   _____

   _____

   _____

2. Write one action step for each of your goals.

3. Which action step will be most challenging for you?

4. How do you intend to keep yourself focused on achieving the action step you identified in question 3?

5. What is your goal for keeping your personal relationships healthy?

PROGRAM STRATEGIC PLANNING

Now that your personal strategic plan is under way, start working on a plan for your program. The process is exactly the same; the BAG and goals are different. Look to your vision for ideas. Perhaps you want the SLP to be "a virtual part of every classroom." Obviously, this outcome is not going to happen overnight or in the next several years. But as you become a virtual part of more and more classrooms, you will ultimately reach a tipping point where even the holdouts will at least recognize the vital role you play.

With your somewhat intimidating BAG in mind, identify goals for the SLP. You might choose "to become an invaluable instructional partner" or "to develop a positive working relationship with the technology department." The latter might be necessary so there are no technological barriers keeping you from drawing on all the resources that should be incorporated into research.

Next, create your action steps for the current school year. For example, if you are working with the goal of becoming an instructional partner, refer to the chart you made of your supporters, neutral people, and those you considered detractors. Are you collaborating on projects with *all* the teachers in the first group? Developing that relationship with them would come first. It is the easiest and will build your base. In subsequent years target those who are less supportive.

The sample page for your strategic plan for the SLP (figure 2) sketches the first year's action plan for one goal. You could put all three teachers in the first cell under "With Whom," or you might work with each one individually. As an additional action step, you could include publicizing your collaboration. Your options vary, from a simple display in the school library to an article in the school's newsletter, a posting on your website, or coverage by the local media. Which of these approaches you choose depends on your school situation and your identified personal strengths.

FIGURE 2
SAMPLE PAGE FOR STRATEGIC PLAN FOR THE SCHOOL LIBRARY PROGRAM

GOAL: To become an invaluable instructional partner

Action Step	With Whom	Details	Completed By	Evaluation
Collaborate with 3 teachers on a project for the first time	Teacher #1	Animal unit	December	Teacher #1's interest in further plans:

Use the same procedure for this strategic plan as you did for your personal one, making sure that you keep checking deadlines to stay on track. At the end of the year, review both plans. To your surprise, you might have achieved more than you expected. As soon as possible after you have completed your assessment of how you did, work on the action steps for the next school year. You want to hit the ground running when vacation is over.

One last concern to consider: as noted earlier, strategic planning is customarily done as a group project. Doing this by yourself is not the optimum method. To overcome the possibility that you are not seeing the full picture or have selected an approach that cannot work, you need to get outside input. Before you go too far in the planning, look for "other eyes" to ensure you are heading in the right direction.

The best possible scenario would be for all the school librarians in the district to work on a strategic plan together, developing common goals but possibly different action steps. Even if that approach is not feasible, ask if one or two of them would look over what you have done. Encourage them to make suggestions, letting them know that "it is never going to work" is not a valid criticism. As Joel Arthur Barker has said, "Those who say it can't be done only get in the way of those who are doing it."[1] Should neither of these approaches be possible, talk to your colleagues in other schools or teachers with whom you have developed very strong personal relationships.

Program Strategic Plan

1. What three or four goals have you set for the strategic plan for your program?

_____

_____

_____

2. With whom will you check out your plan?
3. Write one action step for each of your goals.
4. Which action step will be most challenging for you?
5. How do you intend to keep yourself focused on achieving the action step you identified in question 4?

TIME MANAGEMENT

To successfully add the elements of being a building leader onto your already crowded plate of responsibilities, you must become skilled at time management. You probably have come to the end of a day feeling frustrated because it seemed as though you never stopped and yet nothing got done. What you did with your time was put out fires. You were only reacting to situations being thrown at you rather than working from clear-cut priorities and goals. Although this situation will happen occasionally even with the best of planning, if it happens frequently you definitely need to become better at managing your day.

Charting Your Day

A day has only twenty-four hours, and nothing can change that. However, you can manage your available time to make you more efficient. Before plunging into the details of how to be more successful at time management, do another internal scan to find out what is really happening. Create a form to track what you do by setting up a table in landscape format. Divide the school day into half-hour blocks, listing them vertically down the left side of the page, and put the days of the week across the top. Start with a row for "before school" and end with one for "after school." Make the cells large enough for you to put in several activities (about four lines). Print the form; it will be three to four pages, so staple them together.

As close as possible to the half-hour mark, list what you did during the previous thirty minutes. You might have only one activity, such as "taught a class," or a number of them if you took care of a printer problem, talked with a teacher, made a phone call, and gave directions to a volunteer. Sometimes you will be too busy to record what you were doing at the half hour. Do the best you can to fill it in as soon as you have a chance.

At the end of the week, review how you spent your time. Using a highlighter, identify the activities that were part of your prime focus—that is, your roles as an instructional partner, teacher, information specialist, and program administrator.[2] Star any of those activities that promoted you as a building leader. With another color, mark the activities that had to be done but did not advance your purpose or program, such as changing a toner cartridge. Switching to a third color, highlight anything that was a time waster. This category would include flipping through magazines you like personally or ordering something on the Internet. This is not to suggest that you should never "waste time." You do need breaks on occasion.

Look at your color-coded tracking sheet. It will give you insight into not only whether you are working efficiently but also whether you are moving toward becoming an indispensable building leader. How many stars do you see? If there are very few, you are not as significant a player in the school community as you need to be. Is a high proportion of your time devoted to your primary roles? Those of you on a fixed schedule will likely do well here, but it may not mean much. Most periods of the day are filled with scheduled classes, but few people are seeing you in any role other than teacher. Even worse, some of your colleagues see you solely as their cover for a duty-free prep period. Some of you might believe that covering contractual time for teachers is a job guarantee, but in an economic downturn or a budget defeat, you will likely face elimination. Pushed to the wall to cut costs, why should a superintendent or a board of education save a position that from their point of view does not do much? To offset this perception, you must focus more time on becoming visible in strong, positive ways.

Time Tracking

1. What constitutes the biggest use of your time?

2. Should it be?

3. What surprised you about how you spend your time?

4. What aspect of your program needs more of your time?

Using To-Do Lists

Everyone has heard of to-do lists. Some like them; others think they can manage everything in their heads; and a few hate being pinned down, so they avoid the concept completely. Unfortunately, these lists are a must if you are to accomplish important tasks and stay focused. However, there are several different ways to structure them, allowing you a choice that best fits your personal style.

The most typical way of doing a to-do list is to jot down the items when they occur to you and cross them off as they are completed. Most people expect to finish everything in one day, but there is no reason to hold on to that notion. Indeed, such an expectation is likely to set you up for failure. Consider a weekly list of *only* priority items. That will remind you of where you need to spend most of your time.

Those who get a sense of accomplishment by crossing items off should list everything but plan on taking two or more days. Place an asterisk next to priority items so these do not get lost amid all the smaller tasks. When your sheet of paper is filled with many crossed-off items, start another list. If you keep rewriting the same task again and again, consider it a red flag. You are avoiding something that requires your attention.

Another way to organize a to-do list is by category. Rule a writing pad so that you have a column on the left that is about one-third the width of the page. You might have lesson plans, reports, back room, teachers, and the like, as divisions. This approach helps organize your thinking and gives you an idea of where to put your greatest efforts. You can still star those items that have the highest priority or create this list for multiple days or a week.

When first focusing on time management strategies, keep a list of "add-ons." What did you do that was not on your list? Record the activity along with the number of minutes you spent on it. Was there an emergency that required you to shift gears? Had you forgotten something important? Did you take unplanned downtime? Were you procrastinating? Were any of these a good use of your time?

Procrastination is not an evil in itself. It is a human trait, and it can be helpful. If you did it because you were not truly ready to tackle a particular task, you may have needed thinking time. However, if you are regularly wasting time— avoiding work rather than using downtime to refresh or think—you have to deal with the problem. Schedule fifteen to twenty minutes to do whatever you like, and then discipline yourself to stick to your timetable.

Businesspeople tend to quote Pareto's Principle, also known as the 80/20 rule, which states that only 20 percent of what you do is really important and that this 20 percent produces 80 percent of your results. The ultimate object is to spend 80 percent of your time on that 20 percent.[3] Keeping a to-do list and monitoring how you use and abuse your time will help get you to that 80 percent.

To-Do or Not To-Do

1. What type of to-do list seems to work best for you?

2. What surprised you about how you use your time?

3. Can you identify the 20 percent of your tasks that are important?

4. What percentage of your time are you spending on that 20 percent?

Fitting the Task to the Time

An overlooked aspect of time management is knowing which task to choose when. Going sequentially through a to-do list is not likely to be effective. Most people have a tendency to record major jobs first, then an assortment of things they do not want to forget, and finally whatever else needs doing. Those first items usually take a lot of time, and you rarely have that. Your day is mostly taken up with working with students. In between you have a few minutes to spare.

Think of your tasks in terms of those taking fifteen minutes, thirty minutes, or one hour or more. The latter category includes anything that requires continuous thinking in order to complete. For example, budgeting, particularly at the high school level, needs a large block of time. If you interrupt yourself after fifteen minutes to do something else, you will waste time when you get back to the budget as you try to remember where you left off.

Finding the one-hour-plus time blocks is difficult. Some of you do not take official prep times, and others find your scheduled time is interrupted. You may want to plan on arriving extra early or staying late for these time-consuming tasks. Keep most of the lights off and the door locked so faculty members do not notice you are at work and barge in. This is not the time to be helping them, and yet you want to avoid having to tell them you are too busy. The darkened room should prevent most of them from sapping these precious minutes.

Using fifteen minutes for e-mail, if you force yourself to hold to the time limit, is a highly efficient way of working. You can quickly scan through and delete what is not important, respond to the easy ones, and save those that will take a bit more thought for later. Opening snail mail is another fifteen-minute job. Mail can be put down at any time and picked up later without any loss of continuity. Just keep sticky notes handy so you can mark what should be done with each piece that does not go into the trash. You never want to handle mail twice.

Troubleshooting a computer problem is best kept for a thirty-minute period. If you cannot fix the problem within that time frame, it needs to be referred to the tech department or sent out for repair (depending on how you handle these situations in your district). Writing lesson plans is another half-hour job. Creating a template for them with state and national standards (for both the subject and the information literacy curricula) will take much longer, but once you have it you can cut and paste as needed.

Consider structuring your to-do lists in this time-based manner. Instead of categories, identify your tasks based on the amount of time they take. Remember, a job may really require an hour, but you might be able to get it done in short, fifteen-minute bursts. Going through a reviewing journal is an example. Flag where you stop, and you will have no problem picking it up again when you have some spare moments.

Building Blocks

1. List your fifteen-, thirty-, and sixty-plus-minute tasks.

2. Which category has the most tasks? The least?

3. What can you do to get the big jobs done?

Planning

Although most of your day is taken up with small jobs, the really big ones are what get you noticed. Doing an expansion or renovation project will bring a lot of attention. Automating the school library for the first time or migrating to a new vendor, though less obvious to most of your users, will get you recognition from the tech department and the administration. Your multiyear strategic plan is another large undertaking.

If the idea of a huge project is intimidating or not a possibility given financial constraints, consider something smaller. A medium-sized project may be to bring a new database or piece of technology into your program. Having a new item means little, however, if it is not being used. Selecting the item for purchase is only an early step. You need to develop a plan for integrating the new item or piece of technology into the curriculum. For example, you could arrange a long-term demo or set up a pilot program. Publicity will be an important factor in getting the new item adopted. What media will you use to do this? Print? Electronic? Both?

When you are even indirectly responsible for spending many thousands of dollars, you have a lot at stake. This is where being a leader is heavily about risk taking. Keeping track of the details, alerting the appropriate people when delays affect a time line, and just being sure you do not miss anything requires careful time management.

Look for ways to break the project into smaller pieces. Although there may be interest in the concept, frequently the budget dollars are not there for it to be completed in one year. Always give several alternatives accompanied by what is gained or lost, or both, for each possibility.

Technology has made project management infinitely simpler. It still is not easy, but you no longer need file folders for each month with "tickler" messages. Use your web browser's calendar and "to-do" widgets to keep everything in front of your eyes. For backup, use your PDA. Keep a list of contact people with phone numbers and e-mail addresses so you can reach them as quickly as needed.

Most of all, start gathering recruits. Collaboration and delegation are the key ingredients to maintaining your sanity and coming out looking good. Look for partners who will benefit from the project to be collaborators. Give them ownership of the parts they like best or are most interested in seeing accomplished.

Find people who like to be involved in making things happen or who have special skills. Those with artistic talent can do flyers and other promotional materials. Others love detail work and get a tremendous sense of accomplishment in making sure all the pieces are done. This is the kind of person who can clean files before automating or migrating.

You will not have time to do everything yourself, and the project will get greater recognition if many people are involved. They will be talking to their friends, expanding the number aware of what is going on. Of course, you must check in with all of them at regular intervals to be sure that no one is hitting a snag. Do brief monthly updates for both the administration and your partners and helpers. This accounting keeps the momentum going and ensures that everyone feels connected to the project and is committed to its success.

Successful Planning

1. What medium-sized or large plan would put the SLP in the limelight?
2. How can the plan be divided into smaller units?
3. Other than you, who would most like to see the plan achieved?

KEY IDEAS

- Before you can lead effectively you need to know yourself well.
- Assess your strengths and weaknesses.
- Categorize your supporters and detractors and note which of them are powerful.
- Create a multiyear strategic plan to increase your visibility.
- Develop a strategic plan to achieve the mission of your SLP.
- To accomplish big goals you must manage your time wisely.
- Track how you spend your day.
- Use a to-do list format that fits your personal style.
- Categorize tasks into the time blocks it takes to work on them effectively.
- Design a medium- or large-scale plan and manage it with partners and helpers.

Notes

1. "Inspirational Quotes," www.marksquotes.com/inspirational.
2. American Association of School Librarians, *Empowering Learners: Guidelines for School Library Media Programs* (Chicago: AASL, 2009), 16.
3. F. John Rey, "Pareto's Principle: The 80-20 Rule," http://management.about.com/cs/generalmanagement/a/Pareto081202.htm.

PART II
Knowing Your Stakeholders

Do you know your customers? No successful business operates without that information—or without regularly scanning the environment to be sure that the information is up-to-date—because markets and demographics change. Many of us like to think of *patrons* rather than customers, but that term has a way of smoothing over hard facts of life. You must know what each of your stakeholders values, needs, and wants if you are going to stay in business.

Now that you know who you are and what your plans are, it is time to fine-tune your thinking by recognizing and dealing with basic truths. An SLP does not operate in a vacuum. You are a small, and too often insignificant, part of a larger organization. In order to survive and thrive, you need to be seen as valuable. You already know you are, but you cannot just tell people that your program makes a vital contribution. You must demonstrate value—always. Most critical for you to remember is that this value is not what *you* consider important but what the various stakeholders find valuable. Therefore, to be successful, you need to recognize what each of these groups wants and find ways to show them how your program delivers it.

The next chapters are not arranged according to your priorities. If they were, students would be first. Rather, the sequence reflects the power structure.

Your funding is dependent on the administration and the board of education. They listen to parents because they want to keep their jobs, and parents vote. Do not overlook the community, particularly local businesses. They, too, are voters, and their voices, though not always tuned in to the schools, can be raised in support if you make them aware of how an active SLP benefits them.

Although you think of yourself as a teacher, the faculty may not. Getting your colleagues to see you as an integral component of their instruction is vital if they are to support you when cuts are on the table. Although the chapter discusses elementary, middle, and high school teachers separately, do not read only about your own level. Many of these ideas work for all grades.

Finally, there are the students. They would say they have no power at all, but their parents listen to them, giving them clout. Although they are the last group in this section, they are the ones you work with most often, and the reason you chose this career.

As you deal with these stakeholders, remember that school librarianship, indeed all of education, is a relationship-based business. No matter how important it is for you to know technology and the latest trends in education, what really makes a difference in leadership is creating meaningful connections. As leadership expert John C. Maxwell has said, "People don't care how much you know until they know how much you care."[1]

Watch your behaviors and keep an eye on your attitude. The first rule in successful relationship building is not to make others wrong, even if you are right (*especially* if you are right). Get back to people! Try to respond to key e-mails within twenty-four hours. Do not assume someone is ignoring you because she hasn't answered you in a timely fashion. Cyberspace is not as perfect as we like to think it is.

And some more rules:
- Greet people and learn their names.
- Treat everyone as an equal.
- Do not assume someone is not as smart as you because his job does not require a college education.
- Do not tell people how to do their job.
- As much as possible, ask questions rather than give directions.

Note
1. "Quotes by John C. Maxwell," www.goodreads.com/author/quotes/68.John_C_ Maxwell.

CHAPTER 4
What Do Administrators Want?

Board of Education

Superintendents

Central Office

Principals

Supervisors and Department Chairs

Key Ideas

It will take more than flying to scale this mountain.

SUPERINTENDENT

PRINCIPAL

SUPERVISORS

Administrators comprise a fairly sizeable group. Your principal may be the most familiar and the first one you think of, but you must always be aware of the others. The superintendent of schools carries the most weight and is most visible with the board of education. Do not forget the central office staff—particularly, but not exclusively, the assistant superintendent for curriculum.

Because districts range in size from a single school to as many as hundreds of schools in some large cities, it is impossible to describe specific organizational structures. Despite that circumstance and the vast range in numbers and titles of administrators, there are some overall basics with which you need to become very familiar. (Those of you in urban areas, where it sometimes seems as though there are more administrative personnel than teachers, should focus on the ones whose jobs are closest to what is described in this chapter.) Where present, supervisors and department heads may be of lesser consequence, but you should not overlook any and all potential supporters.

Although technically not part of the administration, the board of education is the official power source in the district, and you cannot ignore it. The board is responsible for setting policies and makes the final decision on all hirings and firings. Whether it vigorously charts a direction for the school district or is simply a rubber stamp for the superintendent, it is the ultimate court of appeals, and its decisions are final.

BOARD OF EDUCATION

As with most people, board of education members want to keep their jobs. Most often it is because they are committed to ensuring that the children in their district get the best education possible and truly want to do everything in their power to make this a reality. Some members have personal agendas they want to advance. One member may be a big supporter of the football team or athletics in general. Another's sole purpose is to keep property taxes down and will vote against any program no matter how valuable if it will cost a significant amount of money.

Although city boards of education are appointed by the mayor, in the majority of districts members are elected. Whether it is the mayor or the voting public who put them in place, board members must frequently choose between heeding their conscience and retaining their jobs. Too often self-interest wins out. What boards fear the most is a lawsuit and negative publicity. Although most school librarians go through their entire careers without encountering a book challenge, and those challenges that occur are most often resolved at the building level, a significant number become local and national cause célèbres and may endanger the job of the school librarian.

Despite your concern about possibly losing your position, you should not operate out of fear and avoid purchasing certain titles to prevent an incident. Instead, you need to behave like a leader. Do everything in your power to get a selection policy passed by the board that includes a procedure for challenges.

You can find help at ALA's Office for Intellectual Freedom (www.ala.org/oif). Click on "Challenges to Library Materials" and then on "Strategies and Tips for Dealing with Challenges."

Once a policy has been passed, prepare a one-page fact sheet that explains the difference between censorship and book selection, parental rights regarding their child's book choices, and other basic information. With the approval of the administration (probably the superintendent of schools), send the fact sheet to all new board members or have it included in their orientation packet. Make yourself available for further discussion if any new member has questions.

The Internet has presented other potential targets for lawsuits. Even with filters in place, these challenges can arise. Fear of potential disputes has caused many districts and their tech departments to use the highest level of restrictions, which tends to interfere with your program. You are not likely to change this situation, but education is the best way of dealing with it.

To gauge the degree to which the board is likely to support the SLP, you need to know how independent it is. Because the job is complex, time consuming, and done on a volunteer basis, many members rely heavily on the recommendations of the superintendent. For the most part this is a wise approach, as most have little background in education. Individual members may, as noted earlier, have personal agendas, and these can have either a negative or a positive effect on your program. Do your best to know who the board members are and where they stand.

In some districts, board members may pay visits to the school and drop in to see the school library. Although you do not want to play politics, you do need to be aware if a board member shows up and to be careful of what you say and do. At the elementary level, you may have a board member as a volunteer. Treat that person the same as other parents, but always be mindful of her or his position. Invariably, someone who sees the school library in operation on a regular basis becomes a strong supporter.

On Board with the Board

1. Name all your board members.

2. Which members have children currently in the district's schools?

3. Are any of those children in your school?

4. How would you describe the board's support for the SLP—positive, negative, or neutral?

5. What aspect of your program would most impress the board?

6. How can you showcase that area for them?

SUPERINTENDENTS

As the CEOs of the district, charged with executing policy defined by the board of education and handling daily operations, superintendents are always watching their backs. In many states, they no longer have tenure and exist from contract to contract, making pleasing the board their number one priority. Although you would like to think of them as concerned primarily with educational issues, far too much of their time is focused on cutting expenditures and putting a positive face on what the schools are doing. Irate parents call them with complaints and threaten to sue or go to the press or both. (Happy parents never call.) Their days are filled with attending meetings and ensuring that reports and documents required by the state and federal governments have been completed and filed on time.

What superintendents want most is to keep their job or build a reputation that will get them a better position in another district. For many, this means keeping property taxes down by limiting budget increases. The SLP sits on a tidy pile of money that is very tempting to cut. You will need to be aware of the pressure points in your community to ensure that many important stakeholders want to keep the school libraries open and functioning at top level. Superintendents are also concerned about the public image of the district, as that conception affects their own reputation.

The job of superintendents requires them to see the big picture, and you are a very small part of that picture. The larger the district, the more likely it is that the activities of your program are far removed from the superintendent's awareness. Too often this is the reason that wholesale elimination of school librarian positions occurs. To minimize this possibility, you need to make a concentrated effort to keep the SLP in view. Normally, these larger districts have a supervisor of media services in the central office, and you also have to work with that person. One effective technique is to look for opportunities to generate press coverage of events where students have created something of note because of the SLP. To further enhance your visibility, invite the superintendent (and your supervisor and principal) to attend the event. Let them know that the local newspaper will be covering the occasion.

In smaller districts, you may have easier access to the superintendent. Some districts have very flat hierarchies and encourage staff members to bring significant information to the superintendent. Always inform your principal and supervisor (if you have one) if you schedule such a meeting, giving the topic of your discussion and the reason you are bringing it to that level. For example, you might have developed an alliance with a local community college. Although you would have informed your principal, *you* are better able to explain the details of the program and the reasons for it. Try to make your appointment on a Friday afternoon, when there are fewer immediate demands and late meetings are unlikely.

Another reason for a meeting with the superintendent would be to suggest a workshop for administrators. As the person who best knows how to integrate technology into the curriculum, you can offer to demonstrate approaches for achieving this integration along with meeting the NETS-A (see chapter 2). Alternatively, recommend a presentation on cybersafety. Inform the tech department of your plans and seek to involve them as well.

Your ability to work with different departments also enhances your position on several levels. Not only will you be developing advocates for your program, you will also be demonstrating that you are a team player. Most superintendents consider team building one of their important functions.

You know how important a mission and vision are for your program; they are equally significant for your superiors. Make sure that any activity you discuss with your superintendent is connected directly or indirectly to what she wants to achieve. Frame your proposals in terms of her mission or vision or both, being aware of any pet projects or interests. Your ultimate goal is to have your superintendent put these events and programs into her reports to the board of education. The more times these programs are cited in the course of the year, the greater the likelihood that your SLP will be viewed as vital to the image of the district.

Speaking to the Top

1. How long has your superintendent been in the district?

2. Have you identified his or her priorities?

3. Which aspects of your program would be of prime interest to your superintendent?

4. What activity could draw him or her into your school library?

5. What topic would you consider discussing with your superintendent?

CENTRAL OFFICE

For many school librarians the central office is terra incognito. The administrators, secretaries, and clerks who inhabit it seem far removed from the day-to-day tasks of the SLP. The only person you might speak with on occasion would be the assistant superintendent for curriculum, but there are others you should plan on adding to your contacts.

Of course, the aforementioned assistant superintendent for curriculum is the person of most importance to you. Ask permission from your principal to copy this person on all memos and reports. But what does this administrator value? Most are planning to move up the ladder and become superintendents in their own right. To build the necessary reputation for this move, they want the district to excel or at least demonstrate regular and significant improvement in high-stakes tests. Your approach should be similar to the one you take with a superintendent. Consider inviting the assistant superintendent to a lesson that connects to the tests and still builds critical thinking skills.

If the assistant superintendent does schedule an observation, go beyond simply giving him or her your lesson plan. Prepare a fact sheet briefly explaining how the activities and instruction you are presenting fit into the larger curriculum, what connections they have to the classroom curriculum, where they show the inquiry process in action, how you will assess the critical thinking involved, and how the lesson relates to the high-stakes test. This extra work sends several important messages. First and foremost, it demonstrates how the SLP plays a critical role in student success. Second, it shows your awareness of key educational concerns and trends. Last, it displays your strong work ethic, your willingness to go the extra mile, and your high degree of professionalism. Such important results are definitely worth the effort involved.

Another key central office relationship you should cultivate is with the person in charge of special education. Accountable to a high proportion of proactive parents, this supervisor is always looking for meaningful life skills activities to incorporate into students' learning. Point out the importance of teaching cybersafety and good searching techniques. Although these students learn differently, they are just as eager to view YouTube and other popular sites as are traditional students. You can build on that enthusiasm.

Additionally, discuss the possibility of training some of these students as library assistants. Such instruction reinforces their basic reading and number skills when shelving books, gives them opportunities to interact with others when handling checkouts or returns, and potentially gives them skills that may permit them to take a job in the public library.

Your relations with the business administrator (who may have a title of assistant superintendent or financial officer) are mainly related to your budget and purchase orders, and most of your dealings would be with the accounts payable secretary. You want to be sure that you do not cause problems. Should something arise, contact the secretary immediately and find out what you should do to fix the situation. It is important to show that you accept responsibility for your actions.

If you engage in a large capital project, such as a renovation of your facility or the building of a new one, you will have more dealings with the business office. Early in the process, sit down with the secretary and learn what steps must be followed and what you can and cannot do. She speaks regularly with the business administrator, and her assessment of how you do your job will be a topic of conversation while the project is under way. You want her to see you as someone who gets things done on time and according to procedures.

In addition to the accounts payable secretary, the central office is filled with other secretaries and some clerks, depending on the district. Although you are always friendly and learn all their names, you should be particularly mindful of those who work for the superintendent and assistant superintendents. Speak with them when scheduling appointments. Always solicit their opinion on the best time for your intended conversation. This connection acknowledges their understanding of the subtleties of their job and will also be helpful in making your case when the administrator is most likely and willing to hear it.

Once you start building a relationship with central office staff, you can also offer to do any research their bosses require. You will be helping them while demonstrating your expertise and resources. In return, they will say positive things about you. This low-level buzz about your abilities and supportive behavior will enhance the reputation of the SLP.

Power Trips

1. Who do you know in the central office?

2. Can you identify all the administrative positions in your district?

3. What one idea would appeal to an assistant superintendent or other central office administrator?

4. How can you bring your idea to this person?

PRINCIPALS

Principals are the face of the school. In today's world they have tremendous responsibilities and not nearly enough authority. At the elementary level, unless it is a very large school, they deal with everything from students to the central office, parents, and wandering board of education members, as well as the secretarial and custodial staff. The principal is supposed to be the building leader and know everything going on within it. To be regarded as a strong contributor to the larger administrative team, the principal must be familiar with educational trends and able to identify professional development requirements for teachers, yet not overlook the need to schedule regular fire drills. Most principals are drowning in details. They put in long hours, and parents expect them to show up for all events.

Principals want their school to stand out and be exemplary, particularly when compared with others in the district. Principals know that test scores matter because if these are low or drop from the previous year, parents and the superintendent will hold them accountable. They try to avoid grievances from unions, maintain a safe and clean building, and always appear to be in charge of whatever situation develops.

Knowing these needs, how can you become invaluable to your principal? Many of you have been quick to inform your principal of studies linking scores on high-stakes tests and student achievement to active SLPs, yet have been frustrated by his minimal interest. From a principal's perspective, everything must be local or it does not count. If your state has not participated in one of these studies, the usual attitude is "perhaps that is true in those locations, but we are different."

If you are going to advance the research results, you will have to demonstrate rather than tell. Try to get on any committee that analyzes test scores and look at which questions connect with information literacy and other skills and behaviors that are part of the SLP. Highlight these and offer suggestions on how the SLP can contribute to students doing better in these areas next year.

Conduct action research to determine your effect on student learning and report the results to the principal. If your research ties to test questions, so much the better. There are several good titles on the topic published by ALA Editions, Libraries Unlimited, the Association for Supervision and Curriculum Development (ASCD), and other professional book publishers. After you have some evidence of how the SLP impacts *your* students, you can follow up with the research studies conducted in the United States and Canada that have previously fallen on deaf ears. Rather than focusing on one or two studies, print copies of *School Libraries Work!* (www2.scholastic.com/content/collateral_resources/pdf/s/slw3_2008.pdf) and give that to your administrator. The twenty-eight-page, regularly updated brochure is well designed and allows for the quick scan your principal will value.

As with the superintendent, know your principal's personal vision and mission. Listen carefully for what is stressed in faculty meetings, memos, and the like, to figure this out. Then be sure you do things that will get that vision and mission realized. You can also offer to conduct workshops that help teachers integrate the latest technology into their classrooms. This effort not only demonstrates that you are a team player but also shows that you recognize the challenges in education and are willing to be a leader in dealing with them.

Help keep your principal abreast of educational issues. Scan any professional journals you receive and photocopy relevant articles. Better yet, if you can make time for it, summarize key ones and send them to her. You should be receiving *Educational Leadership,* the preeminent educational magazine from ASCD, which has themed issues. Even if your principal is a member and has a subscription, commenting on a particular topic of the month is further evidence that you know and incorporate significant trends into your instruction.

Whether or not you are required to submit regular reports, do so at least quarterly. Along with sharing the limelight with teachers and any staff members you might have, be sure to include statistical information. Remember, your principal wants to look good and show what great things are happening in the building.

This report provides that information and will be included in the principal's report to the superintendent, who might incorporate it into his own report to the board of education. (See the sample report shown in figure 3.)

FIGURE 3
MORRISTOWN HIGH SCHOOL LIBRARY REPORT, FIRST QUARTER 2008–2009

Classes

The library hosted over 600 classes and meetings during the first quarter. The heaviest use was by the Social Studies, World Language, Health, and English departments (see chart). The library staff provided assistance that included collaborating on lessons with teachers, providing mini-lessons on information literacy topics, pulling resources, and assisting students and staff with research, computer issues, and finding appropriate reading material. With the growing number of classes requesting the use of computers, scheduling is becoming more problematic. We also take time to plan how best to incorporate information literacy skills into a lesson that frequently has already been designed by the teacher and that now needs to be "retrofitted' to accommodate the information literacy curriculum. Debbie G. and Bilqis provided introductions to information literacy lessons for the freshman health classes. These classes in particular are impacted by the lack of adequate computers, as they are much larger than either computer area can provide for.

Nonclass Use of Library

The library continues to be open before and after school. In the morning, it is patronized by as many as 100+ students, many of whom need to finish schoolwork and projects. It is also noteworthy that although many libraries report that boys do not frequent them on any regular basis, ours attracts a large number who not only like to socialize and use the computers but also read books and magazines. The library staff is kept busy helping students with printer, copier, and computer issues during all these times.

Before school the library is also very busy with the distribution of projectors, DVD players, TVs, and the like. For the first quarter there were over 160 such requests managed by our clerk, Sally. This is a time-consuming job involving receiving the request, locating equipment that isn't returned promptly, and making sure that all components are back and in working order. Invariably these requests also require technical assistance, usually handled by Alison or Jim.

Facility

Several changes were made to the facility in an attempt to keep the library up-to-date and functional. The paperback fiction area was weeded, a process whereby books are assessed

FIGURE 3 continued

for their current value to the collection. Weeded books were deleted from the system by substitute teacher Tony. Remaining books were incorporated into the fiction area, which was completely reorganized by Debbie D. Tony then rearranged the display formerly used by paperbacks to show off many of our new books and began preweeding the next section.

It is becoming very clear that after ten-plus years since the library was redesigned, it is in need of serious overhauling. Technology has changed greatly in this period, and educational philosophy has evolved to view the school library as an active classroom and not just a "drop-in" center. In order to facilitate this changing philosophy, the library needs more computers and designated teaching areas. The current configuration does not promote the best learning environment, and having a technology learning center away from high-traffic areas is a necessity, not a luxury.

Printing replacement IDs is a daily task shared by Alison, Debbie D., and Sally.

The addition of two large, freestanding book displays has been positively received. Sally changes the bulletin boards and book displays frequently, highlighting special events. Debbie D. keeps our student and staff bulletin boards up-to-date with their most recent achievements.

Technical Issues

Network slowness is a continuing concern, as it seriously impacts the functionality of our library automation system. After speaking with the technology director and the library automation company, it was decided to purchase a server for the district libraries out of the high school library funds.

Alison continues to give technical support to staff and students in the library as well as in the classroom. She and Sally cataloged and processed all the books ordered over the summer, which are now available for staff and students.

Circulation

Almost 1,000 books were checked out during the first marking period. We are seeing a big increase in pleasure reading. Several Freshman English teachers are emphasizing reading this semester. Debbie G. and Bilqis are asking for feedback from students to ensure that the library has books that they want to read. Circulation statistics show that almost one-third of the books are checked out by boys. This is an important statistic, as research shows that frequently boys are underrepresented in the library. Circulation figures do not reveal the even larger number of books used in the library without being checked out. All these materials must be reshelved, a very time-consuming and exacting process. Reshelving requires meticulous attention to detail to ensure that books can be found later.

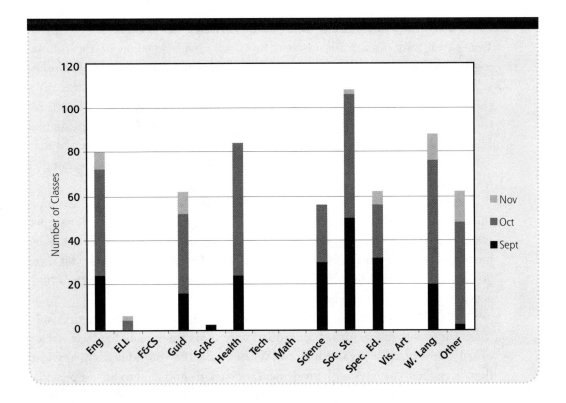

Look for other opportunities to share positive accounts of what is happening in the SLP. Invite your principal not only for events but also when you are planning particularly interesting or unusual lessons. Do not take it personally if she does not show up. Emergencies and unanticipated events are a regular part of the principal's day—much like your own.

In many districts principals are powerful enough to save their own school librarian despite district plans to eliminate the program. Even without that threat, the support of your building administrator simplifies access to teachers and makes your job much easier. Although regular face-to-face meetings are the ideal, they are not always easy to schedule. Because having a good relationship with your principal is critical to your success, make every effort to build a strong, positive one. Avoid whining and complaining. Always focus on solutions and alternatives. Become a partner in achieving your principal's goals.

Principal Issues

1. What do you think is your principal's vision or mission, or both, for the school?
2. What area does your principal struggle with, and how can you help (e.g., technology)?
3. What action research topic would carry the most weight with your principal?
4. What statistical information can you provide that would have the most meaning?

SUPERVISORS AND DEPARTMENT CHAIRS

Because district organizational structures vary widely, some of the following information may not apply in your particular situation. In most locations, supervisors are part of the central office, but because of the nature of their jobs they have a much closer connection to teachers than do the other administrators. In very large districts they are responsible for a single subject area, such as English/Language Arts. Other places give them several areas to oversee but may split responsibilities, having one supervisor for elementary grades and another for the secondary level.

Because of supervisors' regular contact with teachers, you have more opportunities to interact with them than with other types of administrators. What they want depends on their subject areas. Those responsible for tested subjects are most concerned about scores. They will be blamed by the superintendent if these go down. Supervisors in charge of nontested areas want to hold on to their budgets and keep all their teachers.

Do a little research before you begin cultivating supervisors of multiple subjects. Those with a secondary background started out teaching one subject, which usually remains their area of interest. When you make your approach, key it to that discipline. The ones with an elementary background tend to have a personal preference for a particular age range. If you can discover what that is, choose it as your focus.

If possible, set up a desk in the school library where supervisors can get work done while they are at your school. In between seeing teachers or conducting a meeting, they have extra time that they want to use productively. The best place is your back room, although an out-of-the-way area of the floor can work. Having a telephone available for them is also a good idea, but in this day of cell phones it is not that necessary.

You are trying to eventually demonstrate that the SLP can make a positive impact on scores for the subjects tested and show that with your help even areas not included in high-stakes tests can affect the ones that are. To reach that goal, you have to start by building a relationship so that you will be heard. At first, keep it on a friendly basis. While not intruding on their work, you might have coffee and perhaps snacks you can offer to supervisors while they are in your facility. Do not be intrusive. They are there to get work done. Passive hospitality will help you create a friendly atmosphere.

Once you have established a cordial relationship, begin the next phase. As with your principal, show supervisors articles and websites of interest to them. Again, be careful not to interrupt them while they are busy. But when they break for coffee or are getting ready to leave, succinctly provide them with this information. Now you have moved from being a nice person to becoming a valued resource.

Start discussing test scores with supervisors who have responsibility for those subjects. Ask them to show you which ones caused students difficulty and what remediation is being planned. Administrators are heavily into data-driven decision making, and what is taught is strongly affected by identified problem areas. In many, if not most, cases, students can gain the necessary skills in a meaningful way as part of a lesson that you do or that you can do by collaborating with teachers.

Rather than take up a supervisor's valuable time, outline possible units and indicate how the SLP component adds to student learning. In addition to providing a hard copy of your suggestions, e-mail it. Follow up by suggesting that you present these ideas to the teachers at some future date. Depending on the supervisor's preference, such a presentation can be the complete topic of a meeting or a brief introduction that you will use as an opening discussion on an individual basis.

You will need to be very creative to work with supervisors of nontested areas. Once you are familiar with test questions, look for ways other subjects can impact them. For example, the ability to find the most important facts in a passage or compare two different but related items is not exclusive to English/Language Arts. Students can acquire these skills when working on history, science, or world language projects. Learning a skill in another discipline provides the reinforcement that can make a huge difference on a test.

Department chairs are seen mainly at the high school and, sometimes, the middle school levels. They are in charge of one subject and are at the very bottom of the management pecking order. Like everyone else in education, they are hard-pressed for time. Some have classroom obligations as well as their leadership responsibility. Even those who are liked by their teachers hear complaints regularly and are held accountable by all administrative levels above them. A little appreciation goes a long way in dealing with this group.

Although department chairs normally have their own offices, you can reach them by putting notes and journal articles into their mailboxes. Invite them in for coffee and a look at your latest resources in their subject area. Depending on their personal interest, put the emphasis either on print or online material. Offer to give them a one-on-one tutorial of relevant databases and include high-quality websites with which they may not be familiar. From there it is an easy step to suggest you present this information at a department meeting or at a professional development day.

Obviously, you cannot make strong contacts with all administrators in the course of one or two years. This is an ongoing process. Build your skills by focusing on the ones with whom you feel most comfortable. Then branch out to the powerful forces in the school and district.

Reaching Out to Supervisors

1. Do you have good relationships with any supervisors in your district?

2. Which ones are the most powerful?

3. How can you get supervisors into your school library?

4. Choose one supervisor and identify where your program can impact students' scores in that area.

KEY IDEAS

- Know your board of education.
- Invite the superintendent to great SLP events and have press coverage if possible.
- Align your program so that it reflects the vision and mission of your superintendent, principal, and district.
- Identify key players in the central office and find ways to support their efforts.
- Get involved with data-driven decision making and show how the SLP can improve test results.
- Demonstrate, do not tell, how the SLP improves student achievement on high-stakes tests.
- Offer to do presentations for teachers and administrators, showcasing your knowledge of educational trends.
- Find ways to make supervisors feel welcome in the school library.
- Provide small, helpful services for all administrators.

CHAPTER 5
What Does the Community Want?

Parents

- Elementary School

- Middle School

- High School

Business Owners

The Public Library

Community or Other Colleges

Other Community Members

Key Ideas

The community covers a broad spectrum, and, though relatively homogenous in many areas, comprises diverse interests. Although districts to a greater or lesser degree seek to cultivate residents and business owners, voters or those who are or can be vocal are of primary concern to you. You will not be able to reach everyone, nor is it a good use of your time to try. Therefore, focus on target groups, selecting from those most likely to support you and any others with whom you can build relationships.

Parents form the most significant core of this subset. They are the ones to whom you have the easiest access and are the most likely to have strong opinions on the schools and, if you can get the word out, the SLP. In many places they seem to run the schools.

The business community is often overlooked by school librarians but not by the administration. Business owners are a powerful group when energized. Making contacts with them is not always easy, but there are various ways to reach them.

Recognizing that all libraries share common interests, it is wise to become familiar with your counterparts in the public library. Although you do not want anyone to think that what you do can be subsumed within the public library, you do want to show the benefits of cooperation. If there is a college in your area, particularly if you are at the high school level, you can bring greater depth to your program by forming a connection there.

What remains is the rest of the community. For the most part, the people in this group are relatively apathetic about the schools. You need to keep their presence in the back of your mind, as they are often the ones who rise up to defeat the budget and cause tremendous harm to your SLP.

PARENTS

In some communities, they dominate the school and are highly active, but generally parents range from a small, very involved core to those who, at best, focus only on their own children's individual situations. How they view the system and what they want from it tends to vary with their child's grade level. Because they all have a personal connection to the school and are rarely ignored by the administration, they can be your best allies or become an opposing force.

Elementary School

These are the warm, fuzzy years. Parents send their young off with a mixture of anticipation and apprehension. Although the start of school aften provides parents additional free time or the opportunity to return to work, most parents recognize that this is the first big step in a child's journey toward adulthood. Some may be saddened that they are no longer the center of their offspring's universe. All want their children to be loved by their teachers and fear that might not happen.

The open, welcoming environment you create allows you to make each child feel special and appreciated. Although most of you have a fixed schedule and focus heavily on large-group instruction, book selection time is when you can have one-on-one interactions with students. Keep track of whom you speak with in each class so that you can eventually get to every child. Your comments and suggestions when repeated at home give parents a sense of your caring.

Parents want their children to be successful in school. How each defines success varies, but most definitions include being a top student (or at least a good one) and being accepted and liked by classmates. Parents also want their child to enjoy reading. The AASL tagline "Kids who read succeed" resonates strongly at this level, as does "Every kid succeeds @ the library."

Your job is to make sure that both of those messages are sent regularly and demonstrated often. Promote the concept that reading skills are learned in the classroom but lifelong readers are nurtured in the school library. Reading programs lasting a few months and a huge display where interested parents can see how their child or their child's class is doing get their attention and interest. Inform parents of these programs and displays in as many channels as you have available. Among your options are letters sent home announcing the program and asking for parents' cooperation, pictures on your web page showing the progress of this schoolwide activity, and an article in the school newsletter when the program ends. If you create a culminating activity that brings in the local media and parents (and administrators), so much the better.

Many parents have fond memories of storytime in libraries and want the same experience for their children. Use your website to capitalize on this support by posting what you read to the different grades. Provide a synopsis of the books. To make it easier, do a cut-and-paste from bookseller websites (giving credit, of course). Suggest simple follow-up activities whenever you can. Two or three questions or one activity, or a combination of these, will suffice.

Author visits and book fairs, even when sponsored by the parent association, give you additional avenues for sending the message while showing your expertise and the resources of the school library. Most schools make much of Read Across America, as it is sponsored by the National Education Association, but do not leave this event just to the teachers. You need to be an active participant. In addition to using the school library as a venue, after checking with your administrator, consider contacting your middle school or high school counterpart, or both, to ask whether older students can come and read to classes.

A chart showing "What I know how to do" can be used to highlight personal achievements for grades K–2. Across the top of the chart, list the skills and behaviors that you stress. List the students' names vertically. Have the children "self-assess" when they have accomplished each skill or behavior, and fill in the box with a star. Display examples of grades 3–6 research projects, making sure to eventually include each student. On your website, announce whose work is now decorating the school library.

You are probably feeling that there is no way you will have time to do all these tasks. If you are thinking that you need to take on the whole project by yourself, you are right—there's no way. But remember one of the key points of time management: delegate. Consider having volunteers handle this chart. One can select and mount the display (knowing that you want to rotate the featured students). Another who enjoys working on the computer can update the website.

Volunteers are an important resource at the elementary level. Although it takes time to recruit and train them, and some require a certain amount of nurturing, they provide benefits that go beyond getting books shelved and in order. They are your conduit to other parents and to the community at large. Volunteers talk about their work in the school library and observe and comment on how you do your job. Do it well and they will sing your praises—and fight to the death to ensure that you remain in place. They can also inform you about issues of community concern. Pay attention and look for ways to address any issues that fall within your responsibilities.

It's Elementary

1. How can you increase your contact with parents?

2. How can you show parents that their child is nurtured and admired in the school library?

3. What skills and behaviors can indicate student success in the SLP?

4. What projects lend themselves to being displayed in the school library?

5. How will you promote these projects?

Middle School

Many parents have become apprehensive about how their child will fare in middle school. Stories of mean girls and general bullying have gotten widespread notoriety—with some justification. Most schools now have a zero tolerance for these behaviors, but it is harder for them to track and react to the various forms of cyberbullying.

In addition to what the school is doing to prevent various forms of bullying, develop several approaches to educate and inform parents. On your website or via a newsletter, suggest websites such as that of the National Crime Prevention Council (www.ncpc.org/topics/cyberbullying), which has numerous links that explain the problem and provide training on how to deal with it. The Council also has student information at www.ncpc.org/topics/cyberbullying/cyberbullying -faq-for-teens.

Another avenue is to present a program at parent association meetings. Expand the discussion beyond online bullying to include cybersafety. If you have time or can do a follow-up presentation, talk about misinformation and propaganda that students might mistake for credible sites. Although many are blocked during the school day (have them opened for your presentation), kids are accessing these websites at home. Because you cannot be there to teach them how to validate the information, show parents what to do so they can guide their children. This information not only protects students, it also shows parents the value of your expertise. Allow time for questions. Some may suggest a topic for a future program.

Grades take on new importance for middle school parents. With high school looming and college not far beyond, they are concerned about their children's academic success and what it portends for the future. No matter the economic climate, they are beginning to recognize that we are in a global society requiring new and greater skills to compete.

You probably do not give grades, but you can help inform parents of what and how their children are learning by featuring class projects on your website. In addition to noting the grade level and teacher, highlight the information literacy skills and behaviors built into the assignment. Identify the online databases students are expected to access and note that access can be done from home.

Create an FAQ on inquiry learning, explaining what it is and why it is the twenty-first-century approach to instruction. Consider allowing parents to query you online about school library–based assignments and other questions they may have beyond what you explained in the FAQ, adding questions that reveal concerns that others might have.

Although funds are always tight, consider including a parent section in your professional collection. You might be able to get some grant money to do this from your local education foundation. Promote the service through all the available communication channels. If you cannot purchase these titles, at least prepare an annotated bibliography and share it with the public library and local bookstores. Be sure to put your name and the tagline for your SLP on the bibliography as a further promotion of your program.

Caught in the Middle

1. How effective is your school's antibullying program?
2. Whom do you need to contact or inform, or both, before doing a parent presentation?
3. What key points would you highlight in a presentation to parents?
4. Are there other parent concerns that you can address?
5. Which inquiry-based projects should be among the first you feature?

High School

At this level parents seem almost invisible. You might spot them in the principal's or guidance office primarily when their kid has gotten into some difficulty. There may not even be a parent association, because not enough people show up for meetings. They are present in greatest numbers at teacher conferences, followed by attendance at sports and other events in which their child participates.

To reach parents you need to plan strategically. During conferences, lure them into the school library with videos of various classes at work (post a sign where they register to alert them to the fact), or some other draw. For example, offer to give one-time amnesty on overdues if a student's parent stops in and picks up a well-designed, trifold brochure on what the SLP adds to student learning. Also, look for extracurricular activities you can lead that will develop a cadre of faithful parents.

Once parents are in the school library, make sure you have a message that will resonate. Recognize what is most important to them. Safety is still an issue, but they are somewhat less concerned about school bullying and more worried about what is happening on the Internet. They are aware of social networking sites, and some have their own pages on MySpace or Facebook, depending on which site their kid uses. Usually their child will not "friend" them, so they still don't know what is happening.

The presentation on cybersafety recommended for middle school is a good idea at this level as well. If there is no parent association, consider offering a special program on some evening (with administrative approval) or at parent conferences. If possible, hold it either immediately before or after the scheduled conference time. The new problem is that texting on cell phones has virtually replaced e-mail and instant messages. Although parents can select from numerous programs that monitor what happens on home computers, there are still few programs that monitor cell phones. Search for these programs under "monitoring cell phone messages" to find what is currently available.

Many parents do not like invading their children's privacy, but if they choose a program that informs users that monitoring is in progress, it is not like spying. The amount of sexually explicit exchanges on cell phones, both verbal and graphic, makes this a topic parents need to discuss with their children. To more fully bring the point home, show them NetLingo's list of "Top 50 Internet Acronyms Parents Need to Know" at www.netlingo.com/top50/acronyms-for -parents.php.

The other significant want of high school parents is for their son or daughter to get into a good college, or, in some cases and locations, be ready for a well-paid job in industry. The latter is becoming more difficult to accomplish without some postsecondary education. Many parents, however, do not realize they want their children to get through college successfully *in four years*. Few are aware that the average student now takes six years to graduate, and nearly half the entering freshmen do not graduate at all.[1] In addition, parents have no knowledge of the importance of information literacy skills and, awed by the tech-savvy skills of their children, do not perceive any need to teach them anything related to the Internet.

To get your core message across that the range of competencies included in AASL's *Standards for the 21st-Century Learner* is vital and that the SLP is an essential component to their children's future success, you will need to funnel it through the college issue. In cooperation with your school's guidance department (more on this in chapter 6), plan programs on using school library resources to select colleges and be accepted by them. Although many will purchase the various compendiums giving college information, few can acquire them all, while you have these as well as additional material on writing entrance-winning essays and other related topics.

In the course of these presentations, introduce the frightening statistics. Parents quickly appreciate that six years of college costs over 50 percent more than the traditional four (because tuition goes up every year). From there you can make the point that these students are college-eligible but not college-ready. The skills, attitudes, and behaviors addressed in the AASL national standards and therefore in the SLP provide the critical thinking necessary for them to be successful and graduate on time.

Depending on the amount of time you have, you might also want to explore with parents the fact that knowing how to search the Internet or use technology is not the same thing as having the ability to evaluate credibility and select relevant information. Once you have proven to them the value you bring and how you directly contribute to student success, they become the allies you need. If you ever question their power, check out the success story of the Spokane (Washington) moms at www.schoollibraryjournal.com/article/CA6590045.html.

Going Higher

1. What will you do to bring parents into the school library during conferences?

2. What club or other activity can you advise?

3. Besides presentations, what vehicles do you have available to send your message to parents?

BUSINESS OWNERS

The small-business owners in your community tend to live there. As a result, they have a double agenda. On the one hand, they want schools to thrive because successful schools make the town or area (in larger locations) a favorable place to live. This feature tends to result in more business. On the other hand, they do not want their taxes to go up.

Before determining how you can address business owners' wants, you need to consider whether it is a good use of your time, because this group is hard to reach. If you know local business owners, certainly you want to send messages to them that match their needs, but you should not be actively pursuing them. This does not mean you should ignore opportunities when they fall into your lap.

For instance, at the high school level the school library might be used for a visit from the chamber of commerce or local realtors. Rather than complaining about having to close off a section of your facility (or close it entirely) while they are there, prepare a fact sheet or brochure highlighting key points. Your key message is "What the SLP Does for Our Community."

In the brochure or on the fact sheet, prominently include your tagline and mission and vision statements. Select statistics that go beyond circulation figures to include collaborative units or, at lower grades, the number of stories read in a given month. List top examples of twenty-first-century skills learned through the SLP.

Look for ways to partner with businesses, making owners more aware of what you do, but make sure the partnership connects with your program. Readings at local bookstores are one way to reach out without too great an investment of time. You can have your brochure available by the cash register.

With administrative approval, see if any businesses are willing to help sponsor an author visit. In addition to a big sign announcing the fact, try to get the local media to cover the event. The coverage will give the business some free publicity. Even better, when people help you, they become committed to your success.

Once you have made some good contacts, you might be able to address the Rotary or Kiwanis clubs, or both. Because they meet during the day, you would have to be excused in order to attend, but most administrators can support this. They might even join you. This is your chance to let club members know that the SLP is a cost-efficient means of improving student learning, which increases scores on high-stakes tests. These scores tend to be heavily reported within the state and show that your community is a great place to live and raise children.

Again, you do not want to commit too much of your time to this segment of the population, but you should stay aware of it and be ready to promote your program here as well. Remember, some of these business owners may serve on the board of education and even more of them are likely to be parents. They often look for graduates to become their employees. They have a stake in a quality education; be sure they know you are a major contributor to it.

Business Sense

1. What contact do you have with the local business community?

2. Which businesses might want to sponsor an event in the school library?

3. What statistics and other information will you put in a brochure for business owners?

THE PUBLIC LIBRARY

If you are not a community resident, you may not have much contact with the public library, but you and the librarians there have many common interests. The financial well-being of your town or city affects your budgets. The board of education has oversight in the schools, while a board of trustees does the same for the public library. Both boards are made up of locals. In many places the superintendent of schools is an ex officio member of the board of trustees.

You deal with a similar problem in that people mistake clerks for professionals and do not appreciate the need for a college education, let alone advanced degrees, to perform your job. Additionally, you serve much of the same clientele. Students, parents, and teachers living in the district to a greater or lesser extent are public library users. You both promote reading and literacy and often benefit from a state or regional consortium for your electronic databases.

Given these many commonalities, it is foolish not to work together to achieve your similar purposes. The divide that exists may arise from some envy on the part of public librarians and fears from school librarians. In general, the pay scale for teachers—and therefore school librarians—is higher than that of public librarians. They sometimes feel that they put in more hours and work more than the traditional 180-day school year, and yet receive a much lower salary. On the other hand, the jobs of school librarians in some locations are being threatened by cost-cutting attempts that seek to merge the public library and the school library.

A great deal of this distrust can be eliminated or minimized by more contact enabling both librarians to get to know each other better and finding ways to show the community the advantage of your working together as separate institutions. Visits by the children's librarian to the elementary school library happen in some places, usually in preparation for the summer reading program, but these should occur more often so that children recognize that person as a friendly face.

In addition, you should invest some of your time in after-school visits to the public library. You need to know what it looks like, what the collection contains, and what databases are available to students. Resource sharing is another area of cooperation. If you do not have interlibrary loans, look into setting them up with the public library. You can even, with approval, lend your material for student use over the summer.

Although it requires some legal paperwork (fingerprinting and possibly filing for a substitute license), look into the possibility of switching jobs for a day once or twice during the school year. Better than anything, this gives both you and the public librarian an understanding of the different demands your jobs place on both of you. Your time at the public library is an opportunity to present yourself to the general public and promote the SLP.

Just as you are often caught unaware by an assignment, so is the public library. Get in the habit of calling your counterpart as soon as you realize that students are working on a particular topic. Although this is a one-way effort, it builds a positive bridge between the two institutions, and you stand a better chance of having teachers inform you of an upcoming project if they know you are alerting the public library as well.

If your school has a summer reading list, make sure you send copies to the public library. Do the same for any bibliographies you prepare for teachers and students. In locations that hold Battle of the Books competitions, make sure the children's librarian is given the titles as soon as possible.

Ask if you can put up a poster or announcement of events in the school library, whether it is a book fair, a poetry slam, or a schoolwide reading activity. Even if the public is not invited to these events, you can follow up with pictures that show how the SLP is expanding students' love of literature and broadening their horizons. These photos become another medium for you to communicate your messages to the community.

The more you and the public librarian(s) work together, the easier it is to define what makes each of you unique. Look for opportunities to highlight these qualities for the community. You want people to realize that the public library's responsibility is to *everyone,* while your priorities are the students and the curriculum, which includes a strong instructional role. As awareness grows, there will be fewer attempts to put the school library under the auspices of the public library.

Your Public Face

1. Who is your counterpart at the public library?

2. What programs does the public library offer that you should be sharing with your students and faculty?

3. What material do you have that you can share with the public library?

4. Think of past research units. How could cooperation with the public library have improved them?

COMMUNITY OR OTHER COLLEGES

Just as you need to make connections with the public library, high school librarians should reach out to community college librarians. After all, your seniors will be their freshmen. If there is a four-year college in the area, contact it as well.

You want to do this for several reasons. Although colleges do not get their funding from the community, it is wise to take the comments of Jim Rettig, past president of ALA, to heart. During his presidential year he promoted the concept of the library ecosystem, saying,

> I think of our school, public, academic, and other types of libraries as parts of an integrated library ecosystem. If one part of the system is threatened or suffers, the entire system is threatened and suffers. Libraries offer incredible lifelong learning opportunities. No one type of library can deliver learning opportunities from cradle to grave. But through our library ecosystem we offer these opportunities in abundance.[2]

From a survival perspective alone, making this alliance is a good idea, but there is more at stake. Libraries transform communities and, by working together, you can make it happen in your location.

After meeting with the college librarians, see if you can arrange to have one of them address a faculty or parents' meeting, or both. The concern about students not being prepared to meet the academic requirements of college will ring far truer when it comes from someone who deals with overwhelmed freshmen. You then have the opportunity to show how the SLP, in collaboration with teachers, can ensure that your graduates are ready to meet the demands of higher education.

Although the message seems most logical at the high school level, parents and teachers need to recognize that you cannot impart all these skills in the last few years. The thinking habits necessary must be developed from the earliest grades. That is the reasoning behind the Interdivisional Committee on Information Literacy of the American Association of School Librarians and the Association of College and Research Libraries. The joint committee's focus is on preparing students beginning in kindergarten.

Your relationship with local college librarians should expand over time. Consider a field trip to the college library with a talk from the staff there. Students generally are unprepared for its size and even more taken aback by the Library of Congress system rather than the familiar Dewey Decimal system. The array of databases is staggering to them, as is the large number of students not much older than they are working quietly on research.

The field trip can have even more positive results if a freshman or sophomore can talk with the high school students about what challenged her most when she started college and how she dealt with it. For those who had not planned on going on to higher learning, the visit can be inspirational. Do a follow-up conversation with your students to assess what they learned and what they still want to know.

Explore the possibility of allowing high school students to use the college library. See if they can be permitted to borrow books. This privilege is not as much of an issue in those districts where eleventh and twelfth graders take courses at local colleges.

After establishing ongoing communications between you and the college librarians, suggest an idea that will be a real wake-up call for your students. Have term papers that were graded by the subject teacher submitted (without comments or grade) to a willing college professor. The difference between the two evaluations will send a message better than anything you can say.

Report on these visits and projects on your website. Some might even merit coverage by the local media. As your school and community see the benefits of this connection, they will also place a high value on the SLP.

Higher Education

1. How many colleges are in your area?
2. Have you ever visited their libraries and met the librarians?
3. Which group would most benefit from a talk by a college librarian?
4. Which of the projects described would you most want to bring to your students?

OTHER COMMUNITY MEMBERS

What remains constitutes the majority of the residents. Neither parents of schoolchildren nor local business owners, they have little if any connection to the school system. Despite their number, they would not be included in this discussion if it were not for places where school budgets or tax levies come up for a vote.

Most of the time this group does not bother to vote in these elections, but they will turn out when they want to defeat the budget or levy. This is the only opportunity people have to object directly to being taxed. They cannot vote on the national, state, county, or municipal budgets. When they are angry at rising property and other taxes, community members are likely to make their displeasure known at the only place they can.

As a specific group to target, this one is mainly out of your reach. For the most part, you must leave it to the administration and the education association to work on getting the budget or levy passed. You have neither the resources nor the available time to raise voters' awareness of the importance of the SLP.

However, if you have had frequent coverage in local media outlets, you will begin to appear on the radar of residents. Many are public library patrons, and your work there might get noticed. (It is also one reason why art teachers display their students' work in the public library.) Displaying the name and tagline of your school library at various events creates a positive image. Should the day come when your program is under a potential threat, these community members might support a larger, more proactive group seeking to preserve what they know is essential to students' success.

KEY IDEAS

- Focus on groups most likely to support you and your program, but be aware of all members of the community.
- Recognize that parents of elementary, middle, and high school children have different wants.
- Use a variety of communication channels to reach parents.
- Plan presentations to address parents' concerns and interests.
- Design a brochure or fact sheet to highlight information of interest to business owners.
- Develop an ongoing connection with your counterpart in the public library and work together to support each other's programs.
- Reach out to college librarians in your area, seeking opportunities to better prepare students for the demands of higher education.
- Be a presence in your community.

Notes

1. Education Trust: Press Room, "Empty Caps and Gowns," www.edtrust.org/dc/press-room/press-release/empty-caps-and-gowns-new-analysis-reveals-deep-problems-in-the-graduatio.
2. Jim Rettig, "The Library Ecosystem at Work," www.ala.org/ala/issuesadvocacy/advocacy/advocacyuniversity/additup/about/abt_2.cfm.

CHAPTER 6
What Do Teachers Want?

We share the fruits of the tree of knowledge—not that too many people care.

Teachers are your colleagues. You are on the same salary scale and have numerous issues in common, yet many of you find teachers a thorn in your side, an obstacle to doing the job you love and have been trained to do. To shift your perspective and their reaction to you and your program, try viewing the world as they see it. Most of all, teachers want their students to be successful and reach their full potential. You can help them achieve this goal, but first you have to get past the other wants, needs, and habits blocking your way.

Although you commonly lump the faculty together, they are not really a monolithic entity. In addition to classroom teachers, there are guidance counselors and the various related members of their department, teachers of English Language Learners (ELL), special education teachers, reading teachers and literacy coaches, and the school nurse. The elementary grades have "specials" (of which you are usually one). At middle and high schools something of a divide exists between academic and nonacademic subject teachers, as well as some differences between those in tested and nontested subject areas.

Teachers in general want respect. They feel the community thinks they have a cushy job with short hours, long vacations, a too-high salary, and guaranteed employment once they earn tenure. The truth is most work before and long after the school day. They answer to supervisors, principals, and parents. Sometimes it seems as though everyone is their boss. Record keeping is a monumental task and getting worse each year. Despite belief to the contrary, tenure does not prevent layoffs when a department is eliminated or there are across-the-board staffing cuts. Morale has been impaired in many places. Although you do not want to buy into any whining or complaining, you can provide a sympathetic and understanding ear for those under stress.

To work with teachers collaboratively and get them to support you and your program, you will have to build relationships by addressing their wants and needs. Do not take it personally when they do not cooperate with you. They are not used to cooperating with anyone. Although people in business and service industries work increasingly in teams, teachers have traditionally enjoyed personal kingdoms. Once the classroom door is closed, they reign supreme. They do not share much, even with other teachers. Professional learning communities are beginning to change this pattern, but it will take time to overcome an ingrained working habit.

ELEMENTARY TEACHERS—CLASSROOM

If they knew how to ask for it, elementary teachers would like help. You can certainly sympathize with their feeling that there are not enough hours in the day. However, given their propensity for working alone, you cannot just make an open offer. If you are on a fixed schedule, they are rarely willing to forgo their prep time to work with you. Those of you lucky enough to have a flexible schedule do not and should not want to give any of the joint time away so a teacher can complete paperwork or other tasks.

What you *can* do is listen for discussions of current and upcoming units. Look for resources that will help their students learn the concepts better. At the intermediate level, this service includes locating websites and creating a file for the teacher to use. Find out what is being covered in class, and offer to do a complementary project in the school library.

High-stakes tests cause a huge amount of stress at all grade levels. Teachers worry about being judged based on their students' performance, even though there may be a high mobility rate or other factors that affect results. Learn what is included in these tests and see how you can address them within your SLP. Let the teachers know you are doing this. Ask if there are any areas they are concerned about and suggest that you can help during your time with their students.

Although many of you have cut back heavily on professional periodicals, help teachers stay current by scanning any you receive and alerting them to articles of interest. Short ones are best. Have volunteers photocopy these and put them in teachers' boxes with a brief note. If you have not done so as yet, subscribe to free online newsletters. You can sign up for ASCD's *Smart Briefs* at www.smartbrief .com/ascd and receive it daily. It does not take too long to scan through the brief descriptions to see which ones are relevant. However, if that becomes too time consuming, create an e-mail account for your volunteers (you need only one) and forward these to that address. An interested volunteer can be trained to go through a week's worth of the newsletter in a relatively short time. At first you will want the selected articles to be sent to you, but once you are sure the volunteer is doing well with the task, articles can be forwarded directly to teachers.

Edutopia, the website for the George Lucas Educational Foundation at www .edutopia.org, has a wealth of information on innovative approaches in public education. At the top of the home page are tabs for: *Core Concepts*, such as Project-Based Learning and Technology Integration; *Videos* to download that can be sorted by ranking or name; *Blogs* from a variety of contributors; *Community*; and *Schools That Work*. Although there is a fee for the print periodical, you can receive an e-newsletter for free. Become familiar with the website and select a day once a week to do a quick check for anything new. Remember your time management training and do not overwhelm yourself. Again, you might want to assign a good volunteer to do the scan as well as look at the e-newsletter.

The point in all this is to slowly show teachers that you are an instructional partner—one who can help lessen their burden and contribute to their success and that of their students. It is not necessary or even wise to cite the research on how a quality SLP improves student achievement. They will not pay much attention to the words. Put your skills into action and let the results speak for themselves.

Elementary Thoughts

1. Which teachers or grade level would be most open to getting some help from you?

2. What do you think they want or need the most?

3. What areas of the high-stakes tests are proving most challenging for your students?

4. Which volunteers could you enroll in scanning articles of potential interest to teachers?

ELEMENTARY TEACHERS—SPECIALS

Art, music, physical education, computer, and sometimes world language teachers have a schedule similar to yours. The students are not theirs. One after another, teachers drop off their classes at the door and quickly leave to get needed work done during their prep time. In addition to sharing the wants of the other elementary teachers, Specials feel they are thought of as babysitters and not regarded as equals by classroom teachers—just as many of you feel.

Although they teach a specific subject, unlike you who are responsible for a process (information literacy), they, too, see a large number of students each week. They also share your sense of being disconnected from what is going on in the classroom. Although their jobs seem secure because they cover teacher-contracted prep time, economic downturns are proving to them as well as you that contracts can be revised. Therefore, they have begun to realize their need to show they are relevant and important to the overall achievement of students.

Your leadership skills need to come into play here. If you are all having difficulty connecting to the subject curricula, work together on giant schoolwide projects. The music teacher usually is responsible for at least one production during the year, and the art teacher is expected to keep the school decorated, but when you join forces you can create something much more visible.

Plan a project that will last a marking period. You need that much time because you do not see students that often. You may not be able to get everyone on board the first time, but even if only one Special is interested, you can get started. Eventually the others will join in.

For example, you can collaborate on an underwater theme. The music teacher can find songs about the sea appropriate to each grade level, while students in art classes can create everything from murals to collages that fit the topic. Involve the computer teacher by having students create spreadsheets, word process their reports, and utilize other tech skills.

Because few schools have swimming pools, it will be more difficult to connect the project to physical education, but discuss possibilities such as playing tug-of-war with one side pretending to be fish and the other trying to reel them in. Even if the two of you cannot come up with a relevant activity for every week, you should be able to make connections on occasion. If you have a world language teacher at this level, consider incorporating simple songs and stories about the ocean as well as teaching about vacation spots that feature the sea in countries where this language is spoken.

To learn more about what they are drawing or singing, or to find information on places, students will have to do research, which is where your contribution comes in. You can suggest they be allowed to come to the school library if they need further information while they are in a Special. The camaraderie you will develop with the other teachers will make all of you feel less isolated. You might even try for a mini-production on the night of a parent-teacher meeting. The art teacher can get the building decorated, and students can be grouped at various points singing about the sea.

Be sure to show off the research projects as well. At stations around the building, students can talk about their findings as parents walk by to see the display. The combined effort will show how much learning occurs when the classroom (in this case, that of the Specials) is linked to the SLP.

Make It Special

1. List at least three possible themes you could do with the other Specials.

   _____

   _____

   _____

2. Which Special teacher would be most open to such a project?

READING TEACHERS / LITERACY COACHES

It's all about reading. The three of you share the same interest—wanting all students to become enthusiastic readers who can go beyond decoding to get true meaning from what they read. While the reading teacher works with those who need more than classroom instruction to master the necessary skills, and the literacy coach's connection is primarily with teachers to help them learn the latest information on strategies to teach reading to all students, *you* are focused on developing lifelong readers. Building relations with both gives you an opportunity to promote reading in a bigger way, increase your own knowledge, and showcase the individual and combined areas of expertise you bring to student reading success.

Whether at elementary, middle, or high school, work together to forward your common agenda while showing how each of you makes a unique contribution to the overall goal. Share reading lists from ALA and professional journals such as *School Library Journal* and *The School Librarian's Workshop*. Look for ways to be their partner, and have them partner with you.

With the reading teacher, discuss interests and abilities of students and then mine your collection for suitable titles. You can check them out and have the teacher give them to students to borrow, or when you next see any of them say, "I saw this book and I thought of you. Would you like to check it out?" Even better, have the reading teacher bring a group to the school library and together help these students find and check out books to read.

If you have space, suggest the literacy coach set up a section for teachers. Listen and learn. There is much you do not know about the various skills involved in learning to read. By recognizing the coach's expertise, you open the door to additional discussion and expand your knowledge. Use it to match titles from your collection to meet specific needs.

Suggest that one of the literacy coach's model lessons for teachers be done jointly with you, showing the benefits of classroom teachers collaborating with you. Consider going for a joint grant. If one does not exist in your school, talk about the possibility of setting up Family Literacy nights. In these ways you develop a partnership, and because literacy coaches tend to work out of the central office, you will have this additional avenue to promote your program with administrators.

Reading Is Fundamental

1. Do you know the reading teacher and literacy coach in your building?

2. What would be your best approach to working with either or both of them?

3. What project or grant might interest them?

MIDDLE SCHOOL TEACHERS

If you are at a middle school, you and the teachers have a truly challenging job. You are really caught in the middle. The faculty often is split between those with elementary certification and background and those with secondary certification and training. Many of the teachers, and hopefully you as well, love working with students who are changing from children to young adults right before their eyes.

However, in some districts middle school is a dumping ground to which unsatisfactory elementary and high school teachers are involuntarily transferred.

Teacher wants and needs, in addition to those already discussed, depend a great deal on their attitude toward being at this level. Those who enjoy this age group are aware they need to find creative ways to engage their students, whose interests are rapidly changing. The ones who are resentful at being stuck where they do not want to be are looking to make their job easier. Although it is more fun to work with the first group, and they can quickly become ardent supporters, do not overlook the remainder. If you can help them become more positive about what they do, you will at least benefit students and possibly make these teachers recognize that having an effective school librarian available makes their job more enjoyable.

In some places you might be rigidly scheduled (or partially so), in which case some of what was said about working with elementary teachers will apply. Most of you are flexibly scheduled and can get additional suggestions from the following section on high school teachers. But your prime focus should be on recognizing and responding to what middle school teachers want.

Keep as up-to-date as possible with changing technology and what is happening on the Internet. Students can be one of your best sources but so can professional journals. Make time to explore these to see which ones can be brought into research or the classroom or both. Although identifying an example in print is risky considering how rapidly things change, two relatively new tools—VoiceThread (http://voicethread.com) and Digital Storytelling (http://digitalstorytelling.coe .uh.edu)—will probably become increasingly popular. Although these resources have been around a while, many teachers and school librarians have not yet incorporated them into instruction. Yet students love this visual means of sharing information. Finding resources such as these and sharing them with teachers makes you an invaluable partner.

Another example is Skype (www.skype.com). As many of you know, this service allows you to make free phone calls via the Internet. Downloading the software is free as well. Using a webcam, students can talk with their peers in other locations. To bring this technology into your school, you need a plan for how it will be used as well as the support and cooperation of the tech department. On the simplest level, students can work in groups composed of members from another school in the area. You would know the other school librarian, making it easy to get the project organized. Eventually, you might reach beyond the borders of the United States and engage students in global citizenship.

Bringing such ideas to that first group of interested, involved teachers is a natural. They know students pay more attention and become actively involved in learning when they can use the technology tools that are part of their lives. The more resistant group of teachers can be shown these resources after you have completed several projects and can point to what worked and what the results were. If you take on most of the responsibility, you will also be making their jobs easier, which they will appreciate.

Whether teachers *collaborate* with you and are present in the school library while research and online activity are occurring, or work *cooperatively* by giving their instruction in the classroom while you follow up with students in the library, be sure to publicize these projects. Inform your principal and all relevant supervisors of what has taken place, giving credit to the teachers and highlighting student learning. If you can connect these projects to material on the high-stakes tests, so much the better.

Give yourself time. When you are not on a fixed schedule, the only way to see students is to have the teachers *voluntarily* work with you. Here and in the high school this cooperation will not happen overnight. Plan on taking three to five years to create the collaborative environment you want.

Making the Middle Marvelous

1. What do you like best about middle school students?
2. Who are your most enthusiastic teachers?
3. Which of them embraces technology?
4. What online resource or new technology do you think will captivate students?
5. What project can you do with that new resource?

HIGH SCHOOL TEACHERS

At the high school level everyone is aware that these are the last years of childhood—at the completion of high school, students are launched into adulthood. Although they still behave as adolescents, a large proportion will likely go on to four-year or community colleges, with their eyes on eventual careers. Some will head for the military and have to grow up quickly. A few will go out into the workforce without any other training, and some students will drop out. The focus is on making these years count.

As with their other colleagues in the district, high school teachers are burdened by paperwork. Following up absences and cuts by students can eat up much of their "free time." Additionally, they may have meetings with guidance counselors and special assistance counselors to discuss students at risk or coping with addictions. They are responsible for well over a hundred students, and many take on extracurricular activities as well. These activities are not always paid positions, and, though often related to teacher interests and very enjoyable for them, also require a large investment of time.

Most teachers become curriculum and test driven. They do not feel they have the time to pick up their heads and see beyond the next day's lesson. Yet demands are being placed on them to integrate technology, alter their teaching methods, and keep up with the challenge of dealing with young adolescents and all their hormones and attitudes. On the whole, high school teachers love working with this age group, but it can be draining on a daily basis.

What they need is a sympathetic ear, respect and understanding, and help in meeting curricular benchmarks. Increasingly, these measures include higher-level thinking skills that require students to go beyond the textbook. Some teachers consider the resources of the school library a necessary adjunct to their classroom. Others find it a place to relax and read the newspaper or correct papers.

Both groups are not necessarily your supporters. Those in the first often feel themselves quite competent to make use of materials without your help. The second can easily find another place to read. By meeting their needs and wants, you can turn them into allies.

Academic

Academics are usually the tested subjects, although some states test only English and math. Between completing the curriculum and preparing students for these exams, academic teachers feel under constant pressure. Most schools group students by ability levels (which is often a topic for debate). Those teaching college prep classes know that in addition to the high-stakes tests that have been a consistent component of their teaching, their students will be taking SATs, ACTs, and AP exams. Those outside the educational system see the scores as an objective assessment of the quality and effectiveness of teachers. They do not take into account parent attention or inattention, socioeconomic factors, student mobility, class size (which increases as budgets get squeezed), or the impact of students with emotional and other problems not considered severe enough to require special classes. As a result, teachers, particularly those dealing with the less academically talented, can become defensive and frustrated. What they want is more time to teach what they love, have their students be successful, and feel recognized for the job they do.

Unless you have established a personal relationship with a teacher, you will rarely make much headway on collaborative attempts. Your approaches tend to be gently rebuffed with explanations of too little time and too much to cover. Counterarguments you offer only add tension. If a teacher is not ready to work with you, nothing you say will alter that view. Small, subtle steps are the route to changing mind-sets.

Start with the classes that do come to the school library. Even though you were not asked to do any instruction or given any background in advance, you will immediately discover the topic while helping students. As you identify what they do not know and what they need, show the *teacher* the resources that would add relevance and improve student success with the project. Offer suggestions on incorporating them into the assignment. Frequently the teacher will make an announcement calling the attention of the class to what you just shared. When students return to work, propose that with a little advance notice you can prepare materials ahead of time and *perhaps* give a mini-introduction (not taking much of the time teachers worry about) so that students get started efficiently.

When this initial step has proved fruitful, introduce ideas on how to make an assignment more intellectually rigorous, demanding critical thinking on the part of students. Tie this component to "college-ready" requirements, national and state standards, and any curricular benchmarks you can identify. Offer to review (and possibly grade) "works cited" by students. This involvement gives you increased credibility and teachers a helping hand. Your active participation boosts the level of student understanding and accomplishment, which allows the teacher to incorporate deeper content. Then bring recognition by acknowledging the teacher in a brief description of the project and the skills students learned in your report to administrators—including the teacher's supervisor.

Reaching teachers who do not normally bring classes to the school library is more difficult. Lab sciences may never come and, unless there is something in the curriculum that connects to research, there may not be a reason for it. However in locations where schools do not end until sometime in June, AP teachers usually have a difficult time filling the weeks between the exam and the end of the year. Suggest a small college-level project. (Your alliance with a librarian from the local community or four-year college can be very useful here.) Even those who teach calculus and other subjects that rarely if ever make use of the school library tend to be open to your ideas.

It's Academic

1. Which teachers already make use of the school library?
2. What are some resources of which they are unaware?
3. Which academic departments are you not reaching that could benefit from your collection?
4. What project could you suggest to an AP teacher?

Nonacademic

The needs and wants of teachers in nonacademic areas are both similar to and different from those of teachers in academic disciplines. In many cases these teachers work with students focused on future careers along with those fulfilling elective and other requirements. This distinction may be most obvious with the fine and performing arts, but it is equally true for those in the business and physical education (and health) departments. Although the latter is a required subject, it also is a focal point for aspiring jocks and those planning on going into sports medicine and related occupations. Family and consumer sciences now has an increased role in life skills and, in many places, offers training in early childhood careers while being a place for adolescent mothers to leave babies and toddlers during hours they themselves are in school.

The one thing almost all these teachers have in common is the fear of being eliminated. In most places, they have seen shop classes seriously reduced or completely abolished. The next budget cuts could cost them their jobs. They are open to proving to administrators, parents, and the community that they are essential to the overall education of students. Many of them have research studies similar to those of school librarians that show how their subject area contributes to learning or impacts students' abilities to compete in society. You can certainly empathize with their concerns, making it easier for you to relate to them.

With the exception of health classes, few of these teachers are likely to think of research projects requiring your expertise, so a very proactive approach is necessary. Think of topics that can amplify what these departments teach by making global or technological connections. For example, both art and music students can do projects that link to world cultures. Students can compare and contrast other cultures with their U.S. equivalents. Just as you link to subject standards, show where these projects reinforce social studies/history requirements. The culminating projects are natural for showcasing, as they are either art, musical, or theatrical works.

Business departments had been threatened for many years, but more recently the awareness that we live in a global economy has given them greater security. Help teachers reinforce this understanding and consider developing interdisciplinary projects with the world languages department. Use wikis to have students from a language class work with those taking entrepreneurship, marketing, and similar subjects. You might even include students enrolled in web designing. The wiki enables asynchronous cooperation and demonstrates how technology links people in the workforce.

Health teachers are likely to make use of school library resources without any effort on your part. However, as with academic teachers, they are not always aware of the best ones for any given project. In addition to calling their attention to these resources, you can suggest alternatives to written papers. Health classes tend to be larger than those in other departments, and it is burdensome to grade all the reports. Group projects using various technologies for presentations are quickly welcomed by these teachers. Just make sure they do not overlook the need for students to cite their sources, no matter how they impart their findings. Again, you can offer to review what students include in their bibliographies.

Family and consumer sciences has a broad scope of courses encompassing (depending on your district) nutrition and culinary arts, child and elder care, fashion and textile careers, and personal money management. With your coordination, links can be made to other departments, strengthening all involved. Nutrition connects naturally to health; fashion and art work well together; and money management is sometimes part of the business department. To work with early childhood classes, borrow books from the elementary school libraries or get a grant to establish a core collection of picture books, or do both.

The point of this review is that there is a tendency at the high school level to focus almost exclusively on academic subjects. But students will be taking many directions after high school and need to know how to succeed in different areas. In addition, by working with nonacademic teachers you can foster a bond that improves their standing in the educational community and make them recognize how important you are to their continued survival.

Lifelong Learning

1. With which teachers in nonacademic departments have you already done projects?
2. How could these projects be expanded or improved?
3. Which departments have you never seen in the school library?
4. What could you use as a lure?
5. Which of the ideas presented in this section do you think would be easiest to introduce?
6. How will you get started?

ELL TEACHERS

From elementary through high school grades, schools have teachers for English Language Learners (ELL). Often, at lower levels these classes are not part of the fixed schedule, but, as you may have discovered, at upper grades they are frequent users of the school library. In addition to the importance of ensuring that ELL students speed their learning through your resources, you can develop strong partnerships with their teachers.

ELL teachers are under pressure to have their students become proficient in English as rapidly as possible so they can be integrated into regular classes. It helps if you have some material in the languages of these students, but the main focus is to promote English. See what resources the ELL teacher has and look for additional, supporting ones in your collection.

If you are at the elementary level and have some room in your schedule, plan small projects with the teacher. With the youngest students, picture books without words and those with photographs help develop vocabulary and eventual fluency. By third grade introduce information literacy skills with both the Internet and print materials. The former is a powerful tool to use, alluring to students who may or may not have access at home, and encourages them to work hard at dealing with a challenging language. (They can develop their own "dictionary" of words and terms they encounter.)

Suggest to teachers that students research their own country so they can share their heritage with the rest of the school. Although accessing information in English, they will be familiar with the content. Start with the Internet as the lure, but then direct them to books, preferably with lots of pictures. Encourage them to add their own knowledge in creating their presentations and have them analyze resources they find for accuracy and comprehensiveness.

Although you can do similar projects in middle and high school, the particular advantage for the elementary school librarian is having an opportunity to show what can be achieved when you collaborate with a teacher and complete a project over a few days rather than taking a month or so because you see a class only weekly (or even less frequently). With upper grades, research projects can be tied to subject content and be scheduled more frequently. Once students know their way around the school library, they will need only a brief introduction to the relevant resources. Because these classes tend to be small, they can be fitted in even when larger groups are working. Their teachers are generally very willing partners and so will be helping students throughout, and you can deal with the other classes while checking in every now and then to assist with any difficult searches.

The most immediate benefit of working with ELL classes is seeing students become comfortable in using the school library. A secondary benefit that contributes to the recognition of your value to the school comes when the teacher shows parents at conference times what their children are achieving. That acknowledgment, along with discussions at home as students speak enthusiastically about what they are doing, makes these parents strong supporters of your program, and that support then spreads through the rest of the immigrant community.

Breaking the Language Barrier

1. How many ELL teachers are in your building?

2. How many languages do their students speak?

3. Do you have any resources in those languages?

4. What approach can you take to propose a project with an ELL teacher?

5. How should students present their work to get the widest audience?

SPECIAL EDUCATION TEACHERS

As with ELL, districts have special education classes at every level. Even those of you who might schedule ELL students into the school library are less likely to do the same with special education students. Yet they, too, are entitled to use your resources to maximize their potential, and their teachers and parents can become ardent supporters of the SLP when you do so. If you have any personal reservations about these students, take some time to learn more about them and visit their classes in advance of any collaborative projects you do with their teachers.

Special education is an umbrella term for an extensive list of disabilities. It encompasses physical challenges, such as deafness and cerebral palsy (which also frequently presents mental challenges), as well as an assortment of learning disorders from mental impairment (Down syndrome and other causes), autism, attention deficit disorders, and a variety of neurological impairments. The list continues to grow. The paperwork is enormous as students have individual education plans (and evaluations), and teachers consult regularly with numerous support personnel in the district. Many of the parents are extremely proactive in their children's well-being and education and fight hard for all their rights.

Despite their huge workload, these teachers are committed to doing whatever they can to enable their students to be as productive and successful as possible. They are well aware that their students are regarded as different by everyone in the building. Although teachers and students in regular classes become accustomed to seeing these children from their first years in school, a distance continues to exist. To some extent this separation is natural. A sense of "other" is an outgrowth of separate transportation and special classes. Even with inclusion, the presence of an aide underlines that these students are different.

Special education teachers are well aware of this attitude. Although little can be done to change it, they also know their students sense it and want to feel and be seen as "normal." Scheduling special education classes for storytime at the elementary level and doing research as these students get older go a long way to showing they can do the same things as other children.

You will need to discuss these students' special needs with the teachers before you prepare any lessons. Plan to conduct the first ones in their classroom. Get to know the students and let them know you. Follow your in-class instruction or stories with a tour of the school library and an opportunity to check out books. If you can find out ahead of time what they like, you can be prepared with some preselected titles while still allowing them to find others of their choosing.

The school library should already be in compliance with ADA (Americans with Disabilities Act) requirements, but make sure that students with physical disabilities can work at computers and, if any are hearing or vision impaired, that you have headphones and can set fonts to meet their needs. If for any reason your facility does not accommodate them, have a discussion with the principal and special education supervisor to determine what can be done.

Children with HD/ADD, autism, and other such learning disabilities are often as bright as (and sometimes brighter than) those in regular classes. With advice from the teacher on how to adapt them, you can usually use the same lesson plans as you did for other students, which fosters that "normal" feeling these children and their teachers want. The more opportunities these students have to be and work in the school library, the more comfortable they will become, and you may be surprised at how much they can achieve.

In many districts, the special education department has its own newsletter. Work with the teacher on an article for it after each project. You can be sure that parents will be eager to ensure that the SLP continues so that their children will reap the obvious benefits.

Being Special

1. How many special education classes are in your school?

2. With which of these classes would you be most comfortable working?

3. What challenges can you see?

4. Who can best help you resolve these challenges?

GUIDANCE COUNSELORS

Although many elementary schools and most middle schools now have a counselor available, it is at the high school level where you find a full department dedicated to helping students deal with a broad scope of needs. Most school librarians have little contact with guidance personnel, and yet these professionals can be helpful colleagues and strong champions. Once again, to make a connection you need to recognize their needs and wants and deliver what they value.

For the most part, guidance counselors are looking for respect and want to feel accepted as part of the faculty. They are often belittled by teachers who feel they take too long to respond to concerns and questions about students and complain that they provide a hideout for those looking for a "legal" way to cut. College-bound juniors and seniors are frequently frustrated by the time it takes to get transcripts and letters sent. Parents become irate over referrals to school psychologists and how behavioral issues are handled.

In general, guidance personnel are overworked, overwhelmed, and overextended. Counselors are responsible for upward of three hundred students. Those with special needs take a great deal of time—and paperwork, as a slew of specialists may need to be involved. Counselors advise students about schedules and hear their complaints about classes and teachers (frequently accompanied by parents). They organize college fairs, prepare upperclassmen for campus visits, and are often responsible for the security and administration of the high-stakes tests that dominate the educational environment.

What can you do to help, and how can you become partners? Begin with a counselor with whom you feel you can develop a relationship. Make some time to see what resources he or she has and see how your collection adds to them. Share what you discover, and ask if there are other materials that you can acquire that might be helpful. Consider print materials, DVDs, and online databases.

At all grade levels, another avenue for creating a working relationship is to develop bibliographies for bibliotherapy. Students coping with abuse, parental death or severe illness, and other emotionally traumatic problems can benefit from books (fiction and nonfiction) and websites, which are part of your area of expertise. Counselors can give these lists to students, and you can assist further when they bring their lists to the school library to locate items.

By working with guidance counselors you demonstrate your recognition of the importance you place on what they do. Because they, too, deal with budget constraints, they will value the additional resources you provide, allowing them to do an even better job of helping students. In turn, they will champion your services and program with not only the allied professionals they deal with but also parents, new to the district, who visit them in order to find out more about the school.

A Guidance Alliance

1. What resources do you have that would support the guidance department?

2. What are some potential topics for bibliotherapy?

3. With whom will you make your initial contact?

NURSES

Although not usually "teachers," nurses are part of the professional staff. Whether your school is small with only one or large enough for two, you probably know them in a general friendly way. Their duties tend to be outside the purview of most of the staff. Occasionally there will be a critical comment about them not even being able to give students aspirin, but they are responsible for dispensing prescribed medications to students and keeping these secure. They keep track of various chronic and other student illnesses as well as physicals for athletes, usually assisting a physician, and may do training in CPR.

Nurses also keep the faculty aware of precautions that must be taken when an accident causes blood to get on a surface. Of course, nurses are also responsible for keeping records of any reportable accidents involving students and staff.

What you have in common with them (as well as with guidance counselors) is that your doors are always open to students and teachers. Nurses, too, can rarely predict their day, and their job is little understood.

Although there is little you can do to partner with them, and realistically your efforts need to be focused on other areas, they can offer you some help. You can discuss with them recommended medical websites for students and faculty. Additionally, they can suggest reference materials that would be appropriate. Do alert them to any health-related information you have or purchase. These steps are not time consuming and are good ways for you both to benefit from each other's area of knowledge.

KEY IDEAS

- To develop support from teachers, see the world from their perspective.
- Recognize that there are many different categories of teachers, each with their own needs and wants.
- Recognize that respect is what teachers most desire.
- Acknowledge that high-stakes tests are adding paperwork and stress.
- Understand that collaboration—with anyone—is not usually a teacher behavior.
- If a fixed schedule prevents collaboration with elementary teachers, create ways to cooperate with them.
- Recognize how much you have in common with other Specials, and use that mutual interest to create a productive bond.
- Form a triumvirate among the reading teacher, the literacy coach, and you.
- Make connections with middle school teachers by keeping them current with the latest relevant technology.
- Take small, focused steps to build collaborative connections at the high school level.
- Appreciate that lifelong learning skills are an intrinsic part of most nonacademic departments and that you can gain allies by being an important resource.
- Encourage ELL and special education students to become frequent school library users, which their parents will appreciate.
- Develop valuable partnerships with guidance counselors and nurses, who are not usually part of your instructional connections.

CHAPTER 7
What Do Students Want?

We come in lots of shapes and sizes, but we all need you to help us succeed.

Students are the center of all that you do. They are your most important stakeholders even though their influence is indirect. In and of themselves, they have little power. However, their parents, as noted in chapter 5, most definitely do. Although they may see your *facility* at meetings or conference time, parents' awareness of the *SLP* comes through their children. They probably will not notice a poor or ordinary program, but they recognize an exemplary one (mostly based on what their children say and do regarding the SLP and you). When they do, they fight to keep it. Recognizing this reality does not mean you have an ulterior motive in dealing with students. You strive to have them become lifelong readers and learners, comfortable in any type of library and skilled in using information resources, whether current or still to come. The fact that parents are supportive when they see evidence of this growth in no way suggests that you are playing politics when you give students what they want and need.

At all grade levels, students want and deserve respect and fairness. They wish to be treated as though they are important to you and to know that you do not play favorites. On the surface this request seems simple enough, but they are quick to see when you do not value them in the same way you do adults. They observe whether you give "good students" a break or are harder on those who do not always meet your standards. It is important for you to monitor your behavior and attitudes to see how students might perceive your actions.

Treating the more obstreperous students with respect and fairness does not mean you overlook unacceptable behavior. However, the rules you establish should apply equally to everyone. You cannot give a normally good student a break while holding hard and fast to a rule when others cross the line. Likewise, if you do not permit drinks in the school library, you cannot permit teachers to bring their coffee. (Gently suggest that they take it into your office until they are finished.) Students most definitely care less about what you say, responding much more to what you do.

It is best to keep rules simple and positive. Suzanne Savidge, an elementary school librarian in Manalapan, New Jersey, has only three: respect yourself, respect others, and respect the school library. That covers any situation and allows you to remind a student who might be talking too loudly that she or he is not showing respect to others. Similarly, horseplay can be seen as not in keeping with any of those three rules.

Classroom management is a vital skill when dealing with large groups. Although you handle it differently depending on the age you are working with, you must always be in charge. Perhaps surprisingly, all students want this. They feel more comfortable knowing what is expected—even if they decide to challenge you. Your confidence in knowing how to respond and deal with whatever comes up goes a long way to minimizing discipline problems.

PRIMARY STUDENTS

Your curriculum at this level focuses on literature, although it is important to begin information literacy and critical thinking skills from the beginning. However, any curriculum must be set against a background of creating a welcoming, nurturing environment that invites children to want to come to the school library. In most districts, you have a fixed schedule and see classes once a week or less. You want this time to be their favorite Special. You have competition from art, music, physical education, and possibly computer classes. How do you rate?

If you want to be students' number one choice, you have to meet their needs and wants, just as you do with other stakeholders. Consciously consider what these are and be careful that your actions do not send an impression counter to your good intentions. Before putting a rule in place, think how it might be interpreted by children.

Kindergarten Students

Although many kindergartners have been in nursery school and preschool, being with much older students on the school buses and in the halls and lunchroom can be intimidating at first. They are still teetering between wanting to be with Mom and wanting to be all grown up. They miss the love and unconditional acceptance they get from their mother, so it helps if you can supply some of that. Many places, in response to concerns about sexual predators, do not permit you to hug students. But you can always pat a back or gently squeeze a shoulder to show support or concern.

A huge change occurs between kindergarten and first grade as children become socialized to school rules and behaviors, confident in their ability to be part of this environment. You are one of the catalysts in this transformation. Even if these students have become accustomed to being in a classroom, the school library looks different, and conduct they may have learned from their teachers' expectations or from their nursery school days does not seem to apply. It is up to you to set up procedures to quickly settle them. However, always take into consideration their physical and emotional needs. If you do not, discipline will be a constant tug of war.

Structure helps students control their behavior. Establish this even before you orient them to the school library. As often as possible, greet students as they walk in. Smile as you do so. Make comments to them, such as complimenting a particular article of clothing they are wearing, or their smile. By being at the door (and not engaging in a discussion with the classroom teacher), you are monitoring behavior from the first.

You will want to have books returned as students enter. Get the class seated as soon as possible. Unless your furniture is very well suited to their small bodies, have them sit on the rug or mats that you keep for this purpose. Chairs that are too high only encourage twisting, squirming, and falling off (on purpose). They can't fall off the floor. If they are to be in chairs, have these arranged the way you want them before the class arrives. Havoc ensues if you ask students to move their chairs into position. Consider getting seated the opening segment of your lesson and congratulate the class for its behavior.

You now segue into the middle section of your lesson, which is the instructional portion. Set the tone for storytime by posing a question related to the theme. Usually a few students make nonrelated comments about something on their minds. This commenting will also happen if you ask them about something occurring in the story. A good way to deal with a non sequitur is to suggest that the two of you talk about the topic later and then re-ask that student the question.

Make sure all students can see the pictures while you are reading. Although the selection may seem appropriate for kindergartners, observe their reactions. If they are moving around too much, it is your fault, not theirs. The story is not engaging them or it is too long, or maybe both. Stop immediately and ask questions to find out how well they have been following the story. If they are not understanding what is happening, summarize the remainder of the tale, flipping quickly through the pictures, then start with a backup book that you have handy. If you have only a few "itches" in the audience, direct your queries to them and get them refocused. Do not scold them—it tends to be counterproductive.

Attention span is limited at this age (some say this is true through high school), so plan activities to get the children up and moving between sitting times. This chance to move around is particularly necessary for boys, but even girls benefit from the change of pace. Increasingly, kindergarten has more instructional and less play time. Test preparation has eliminated the delight and *learning* that is part of play. Although play should be connected to the theme of your lessons, give them back some time to be young children. You will need a signal that gets the class restored to order and their seats, but if you are consistent, they will become accustomed to responding and settle down quickly.

Finding books is often the highlight of the library period. Hopefully, you have clear sight lines so students know you can see them at all times. Before you send them to the shelves, remind the class that only walking is permitted in the school library. If someone is behaving inappropriately, walk over and speak quietly to that one person.

It is easy to be restrictive, knowing that a title is far too difficult for a student. But for children attracted to a cover or drawn to a sports book, being told they cannot take it out dampens their enthusiasm for reading. Allow it to happen, but suggest they take another book as well. Have a note ready to slip into the book as a marker, alerting parents to the child's choice. This way parents know that you are supervising and care enough to communicate with them, and they will understand that you do this to encourage a love of books.

Checkout time can become chaotic if you do not have a routine. Volunteers can be a big help here. Usually, the best way is to have students sit with their selections and then call up one group at a time. Choose groups randomly rather than giving preference to the "quietest" table or group. That type of reward does not reflect an understanding of where they are developmentally. You can turn the choice into a reinforcing lesson by picking a letter of the alphabet and asking which table or group has an author whose last name begins with that letter. Make it fun instead of a reward/punishment situation.

One of the more pervasive counterproductive practices is not permitting a child to check out a book if she or he has not returned one. If your aim is to train students to obey rules, then such a practice makes sense. But if you are truly committed to developing lifelong readers, you are working against your core purpose. It is far better to put in a bookmark-sized reminder slip that a book has not been returned. Include your telephone number or school e-mail address, or both, so parents can get in touch with you concerning the overdue.

Knowing Your Kindergartners

1. Have most of your kindergartners been in nursery school or preschool or both?

2. What words of support and encouragement do you use?

3. What routines do you have in place? Are they appropriate for kindergartners?

4. What indicators have you observed that tell you students have become disinterested?

5. How do you handle their lack of interest?

6. How do your furniture and floor plan help or hinder managing these students?

First and Second Graders

Although they are still young, children in first and second grade have become far more sophisticated than kindergartners. By now, these students know school routines and behaviors. They do not worry about getting lost in the halls or getting on the wrong school bus. You can already see social demarcations. The popular girls are sought after as seatmates. Boys show some deference to those they view as leaders. If you were able to fast forward to high school, most of them would be occupying their same positions.

Also emerging are the underachievers and the troublemakers. Often these are the same students, which makes a good deal of sense. Every day they are faced with instances that tell them they are not as good as other children. They believe this judgment, and it makes them angry and resentful, leading to behavior issues. You can help change the course of a child's life by proving the AASL statement that "every child succeeds @ the library."

Keep an eye out for those first and second graders who are beginning to think of themselves as losers. Look for opportunities where they can succeed and shine. See what books they like. Those titles may suggest a subject area in which they are interested. Ask them questions about that topic and let them know when they have taught you something. If one is talented in drawing, ask that child to create something for a bulletin board. Give these children a chance to be in charge. That rarely happens in their world.

The more often you can show these children that they can be successful, the sooner they will come to consider it a real possibility. Achievement is more rooted in self-belief than is taken into account in the learning process. When students believe they can, they are able to cope with setbacks. By contrast, those who feel like failures see every stumbling block as proof of being incapable. Follow the practices of good teachers and send success messages home to parents.

If you have one or two students who regularly cause problems, check with their teacher to find out if they behave similarly in class. Perhaps the teacher has developed an effective technique for dealing with them that you can use or adapt in the school library. You might discover that there are some underlying emotional or even physical issues of which you were not aware. Sometimes, it is easy to forget that teachers are your colleagues and can be a support for you, just as you support them.

Although literature is still central to your curriculum at this grade level, begin simple research projects as early as midway through first grade. By this time most students can read sufficient text to locate information, and there are some websites that they can manage. Have them work in pairs, pooling their findings for a classwide presentation.

For example, students can create an ABC book around a theme. Introduce the concept by reading one and discussing where they can locate information. Save difficult letters (q and x and sometimes y and z) for the end, not assigning them to any one group. In addition to the basic sentence "A is for _____," have students write one or two sentences explaining their findings or the term itself.

When groups have completed their assigned letters, have the class work together to figure out how to deal with those difficult ones at the end of the alphabet. Show them other ABC books so they can see what solutions authors have used. With a little guidance they will find ways to complete their book.

From the first, have students record the author, title, publisher, and copyright date so they begin to learn about citations. Explain that it is important for people to know where information comes from so they can be sure it is accurate.

You will be laying the groundwork for more detailed discussions on plagiarism and intellectual property in later years.

You can also have a group work on making an index for the book. By discovering how to do it for their own creation, they will understand the concept far better than any instruction you can give them on how to use an index. The lesson is both authentic and relevant and so learning occurs quickly and naturally.

In the past, you would have put the class book on display, possibly circulating it overnight to each student. Now you can scan it into the computer and make the file available on your website, or you can do a podcast with each group reading its letters. Let parents know how they can view or listen to their children's work.

Early Success

1. Can you identify the popular students in your classes?

2. How do the underachievers behave in the school library?

3. List at least three interests or talents these students have.

_____

_____

_____

4. What topic can you use for a beginning research project?

INTERMEDIATE STUDENTS

Between third and fifth grade, students do not change that much. Their bodies become taller; their reasoning becomes more sophisticated, but they do not experience the major emotional (and mental) shift that occurs in primary grades nor the pubertal disparities that typify middle school. The nice and easy growth from one year to the next allows you to focus on developing their critical thinking skills and encouraging them to use their new reading fluency to build a lifelong habit.

These students want you to recognize they are no longer babies. After-school activities occupy an important part of their lives. Both girls and boys are more sure of themselves and bring confidence and enthusiasm to new challenges, particularly if your projects reflect their interests.

You can foster their self-appreciation by how you structure your lessons. Give students an opportunity to set rules (although the three "respects" first introduced with younger students can and should be a part of that). Have them help you by putting returned books onto a cart divided by Dewey number to speed later shelving.

If teachers are agreeable, you can establish a group of library helpers. As a reward for completing class work, students can be allowed to come to the school library to shelve books, put the facility in order, and even check in books. You will have to schedule training time, and "council members" should be required to sign in and check off what they did on a chart you prepare for that purpose. Let parents know if their child is participating, stressing the learning that occurs while students perform this service.

Although intermediate students are eager for and enjoy doing research, completely eliminating storytime will have a negative effect on their reading for pleasure. You do have to follow your curriculum, but on occasion read a book to the class over the course of a few weeks. Have someone recap the story each time you reconvene. Keep track of factual information included in the plot and do a five- to ten-minute "challenge" at the end of the period in which students verify the book's accuracy. In this way you can still address topics in the SLP while having some time to promote reading. Add a few booktalks on themes in which students have expressed interest. Send home a bibliography of what you featured along with additional titles or post it on your website, or do both.

Research is best if it ties into what is being studied in class. This gives students their first opportunity to go beyond the textbook and explore aspects of interest to *them*. Unlike with the primary grades, groups can now consist of three or four students.

However, before beginning classroom-related projects, discuss your plans with teachers. Most will be glad to have learning reinforced, but others might want to have full control over how a unit is covered. If you encounter resistance, brainstorm with students to select a topic for them to investigate. Sometimes this approach is just as good because it will give them an opportunity to research something they care about, showing them that learning is not only what occurs in the classroom.

Into the Intermediate Years

1. What interests do your students have outside school?
2. How can you use these interests to increase students' learning?
3. What tasks could you give to "library helper" students?
4. What books are short enough to read in a few weeks, of interest to boys and girls, and have "facts" that can be checked?

MIDDLE SCHOOL STUDENTS

Although grades 3 through 5 display only incremental changes, middle school students undergo extreme spikes in physical and emotional growth. Within the same grade level there are those who are very much like intermediate students, while others are experiencing the swings typical of early adolescence. Girls and boys who had preferred staying away from each other now become more aware of the opposite sex. Social tensions are a continuous undercurrent.

Although girls tend to develop faster, some are far slower in their growth. Although the disparity among males is greater, those of both sexes who feel their physical development is lagging often become insecure, and self-esteem drops. As noted earlier, parents are aware of "mean girl" and various other forms of bullying and are justifiably concerned.

All this is happening against a backdrop of leaving the self-contained environment of elementary school. Instead of a single-classroom teacher for most of the day, students now have several different ones for academic subjects in addition to music, art, physical education, and others. In most places, for the first time you are not part of their regular schedule.

Recognize you are in a unique position to be a caring adult as well as their school librarian. Students do not feel as closely supervised in the school library as they do in the classroom. Be very observant of social interactions. Does one student habitually work alone or seem to hide in the stacks? Have you overheard a catty comment made about a girl? Eavesdrop unobtrusively when you note whispering and tittering among the popular girls. If you are alert, you can spot the signs of bullying and identify the perpetrators and their victims.

Discuss what you believe you have seen with guidance counselors, and make sure you are well aware of the school's policy on bullying. Follow all recommended procedures. Also reach out to those students who are the targets. Kind words, suggestions about books, and possibly even having these students become library volunteers can help bolster sagging self-esteem. Do not try to "fix" them. What they most need to hear from you is that you see their worth and value them as people.

Academically, middle school is the real introduction to high school. In many districts, eighth and even gifted seventh graders take what used to be high school–level courses. Most commonly these are algebra and geometry, but students may also get a leg up on world languages, completing their first year while still in middle school.

Although these students have been surfing the Net for years, some since preschool, they are not as blasé as those in high school and are open to listening to you. Because you are most likely flexibly scheduled, you see them when they are working on a research assignment for class. Show them how to reduce the overabundance of nonrelevant sites and guide them to great websites you have discovered through your connection to ALA/AASL and your state association as well as professional journals.

Be open to learning from your students, and they will be even more likely to pay attention to what you have to say. Ask them for recommendations for magazines to which they would like you to subscribe. They are also a great source for suggesting graphic novels (however, you might have to discuss whether these are appropriate for school use) and fantasy series. Although you recognize they still have a long way to go, if you treat them as "almost adults" they will like coming to the school library.

If the district (and the teachers' union) does not object, open the school library to students as soon as you arrive and keep it open after school for as long as possible. Because you are doing this as a service, discipline is not much of a problem. Students should know that if they are not behaving appropriately, they will be asked to leave.

Classroom management is a bit more challenging at this level. During orientation, have students talk about what they consider appropriate behavior. You can still use "respect yourself, respect others, and respect the school library," but you want them to have ownership of the facility and the program. After all, it is there for them.

Because teachers accompany students, you need to work with their varying levels of strictness. Create a baseline for what you consider acceptable and unacceptable practices. The school library is *your* room, after all. If you feel a class is being permitted too much leeway (or, more rarely, being forced into a too-rigid structure), speak with the teacher privately and reach an agreement. You never want to contradict a teacher's style or rules in front of students. They are watching and will use it in the same way they play their parents against each other. You and the teacher need to present a united, consistent front.

Most of all, you want to demonstrate in words and actions that you enjoy working with this age group. Too many teachers are unhappy at being assigned to middle school. Be one of those who truly likes being a part of this huge transition time.

Middle Management

1. What is your school's policy on bullying?
2. Do you know the procedures to be followed if you identify this behavior?
3. What are some telltale signs you have noted that indicate a student is being harassed?
4. How often do you open the school library early? Keep it open after school?
5. How would you approach a teacher who lets students act out in the school library?

HIGH SCHOOL STUDENTS

So close to being grown up and yet so far! Between ninth and twelfth grades, high school students undergo a transition as great as that from kindergarten to first grade. The entering class is not much different from how they were in middle school. Although eager and excited about entering this final phase of education before heading off to college, the military, or jobs, there is some trepidation about once again being at the bottom of the heap. By the time they graduate, many of these students are legal adults and, to a great extent, focused on their future.

What these students want is the recognition that they are nearly full-grown, entitled to their opinions, and able to make their own decisions. Although this is not a fully accurate assessment of their capabilities, it is what they believe. The difference between their perception and yours means you need to be aware of what *they* think even as you guide them into more sophisticated reasoning and prepare them for the realities of what they will be facing after graduation.

You can joke with students and develop an easy camaraderie with them, but you should never become their friend. They have enough of those. What most also want and need is a trusted adult who cares about them. Because the school library is an informal setting compared with the classroom, it is easy for them to find time to talk with you, while you can frequently spot the ones who could use a quick pep talk or ego boost.

These four years are filled with emotional extremes and academic pressures. Strongly emerging sexuality creates tension in relationships. Sometimes students become intimate out of curiosity as much as because of their feelings for one another. Other times, students of either gender may feel pressured into intimate situations. Breakups are painful, and sometimes public. Many students are unable or unwilling to talk about these topics with their parents.

Although they should go to their guidance counselors, not all are willing to do so. Most seek advice from friends, but if you have good relationships with them, a number will speak to you as well. You cannot lecture or talk down to them. As noted, they wish to be regarded as adults. Be prepared with print and online sources, and get any additional background you need by talking with counselors to know the best way to advise students facing these and other quandaries.

Aside from dealing with emotional issues, adolescents are faced with high-stakes tests that may keep those on the bottom from graduating while the college-bound face the tension-producing SATs, ACTs, AP exams, and college entrance applications. Lower-achieving students drop out or act out or both, angry at a system that has decided they have little or no academic potential. Keep that in mind when you are faced with discipline issues, and work with teachers to make research assignments as relevant to their lives as possible.

When dealing with those headed for further education, highlight the college-necessary skills embedded in a project. In addition to suggestions made in chapter 5, if you have developed a connection with local college librarians, have one of them speak to classes about research problems many freshmen typically face. Once students realize you are a valuable source of information on what they need to know to be successful in college, they will pay more attention to what you have to say. They will also let their parents know how you are preparing them.

Prominently display print resources on colleges, the major entrance exams, and financial aid (in addition to what is available in the guidance department), and books on writing essays and preparing for interviews. Post helpful online sources on your website. Also feature information on careers in the military. You want to recognize all the possible futures your students might be considering.

Managing the environment of the school library is often complicated by having one or more classes working on projects while other students come in on passes from classrooms. Lunch periods can become even more challenging when classes are going on simultaneously. Some school librarians restrict the number of students who can enter from lunch, requiring the passes to be picked up prior to the start of the school day. Although this practice encourages planning on students' part, it can be a barrier if the need arises during a morning session. Ultimately, the decision about how to handle this time period is up to you and administrators, but consider getting input from students.

Discuss the situation during orientation or even with students in the National Honor Society or student council or both and see what solutions they devise. Rules that are student-created give them ownership and are much more likely to be followed. Noise levels and eating in the school library are other topics that benefit from having students contribute to what is considered appropriate behaviors.

Food in the school library is a particularly hot-button issue. Most adults have a knee-jerk reaction that it must not be permitted. Of course, they do not mean that there should not be food when adults have meetings in the school library. The double standard is very apparent to students and needs to be looked at closely. Many public libraries now have vending machines in them and do permit eating and drinking from closed containers. Perhaps different restrictions should be applied to areas where there are computers.

Keeping the school library environment student-friendly and yet orderly requires an ongoing assessment of how procedures are working and where tweaking is needed. Class management is guided, but not controlled, by teacher policies. You still need to maintain your standards and expect students to follow the rules they helped establish.

When working with large groups, be aware of when they have tuned you out. High school students believe they know everything about research and are prepared to be bored during orientations. Turn the tables on them and have them tell you what they know. Start a research project by giving little or no introduction, and then gather them back together after about fifteen minutes to report on their success or difficulties or both. When they think they have found a good website, challenge them to prove it is authoritative. If they really do know what they are doing, your instruction would be a waste of their time. Of course, to their surprise, they are less capable of academic research than they thought. Once they realize that fact, they are ready to listen.

When high school students respect your advice, both as a teacher and as a caring adult, they become staunch advocates of you and the SLP. Many of them have become activists for various causes that have meaning for them. If they value the SLP, they will not let it be eliminated without a fight. And the media love to interview students.

The Final Four

1. Do you prefer working with under- or upperclassmen?

2. What are some groups and cliques that you observe in the school library?

3. How do you spotlight areas of your collection of interest to students going on to college?

4. What do you do for those bound for the military or the workforce?

5. What rules do you have that can be seen as arbitrary on closer inspection?

6. What changes can you make to alleviate challenges presented by the lunch schedule?

7. How can you promote student ownership of the school library and their learning?

SPECIAL AND COCURRICULAR PROGRAMS

From schoolwide reading programs to author visits and a host of other possibilities, you can use special programs to broaden student learning and get the word out about the value of the SLP. In middle and high schools, you can become involved in cocurricular activities that extend the reach of your program into a more informal setting. Both types of programming are meaningful to students but also show that you are a leader and an asset to the educational system.

Special Programs

Although in many locations, accelerated reader and similar programs are thought of as the main way to encourage pleasure reading, there is much debate on how successful these are long term. At the elementary level, a great way to generate excitement about reading is to create a schoolwide reading activity. Do one or two each year. If Read Across America is a big event in your school, latch onto it to piggyback on existing interest.

To get started, design a display around a theme—space travel, the United States, the world, underwater, and the like—and then have a color-coded method of graphically depicting the number of books read by the different classes. A talented volunteer can do most of the artwork involved.

For example, students can "read around the world" by looking for books set in different places. Create a bulletin board with a world map as the background. Use one shape (circles, stars, squares, triangles, etc.) per grade level with different colors for each teacher. Those in Mrs. G's first-grade class may have red circles, while first graders in Ms. R's class have yellow ones. As students complete a story (or have it read to them), they write their name on the appropriate shape and color and paste it onto the correct country. Just looking at the display shows which grade and class are reading the most (but not which particular student). The element of competition gets them excited, and the books do the rest.

Sending letters home to parents makes them aware of the program as well as raising their consciousness about what the SLP is doing to promote reading. For the youngest grades, you want parents to participate by reading to their children who are still not ready to do so on their own. This gets parents involved in a more active way and heightens their appreciation for your commitment to developing reading as a lifelong habit. Watching their children take books with them wherever they go further increases parental approval of the SLP. After six to eight weeks, bring the activity to a close. Invite parents to a culminating event in which all the shapes are removed from the display and counted. A media presence makes the impact even better.

Book fairs, whether run by you or the parent organization, offer another chance to inform parents of your value to their children. Those volunteering to assist see you at work, but you can also send home lists of your "top picks" by grade level—or set up a display of them if the fair coincides with back-to-school or conference nights when parents can attend and shop. Although books will carry stickers indicating whether they are Newbery or Caldecott Medal winners, consider identifying those that have been named Notable Children's Books by the Association for Library Service to Children. If you do not have time to do this, post the Children's Notable Lists from the ALA website (www.ala.org/ala/mgrps/divs/alsc/awardsgrants/notalists/index.cfm).

Author visits, which may be virtual as well as in person, have typically been an elementary event, but middle and even high schools are beginning to schedule them. At the lower levels, prepare students well in advance by using storytime to acquaint them with the author and have them write lists of meaningful questions. Inform parents of the preparations being made and explain how the questions students are generating help them develop critical thinking and analytical skills.

Further prepare students by directing them to the website of the visiting author. With this additional background, they discover facts about the author's life, themes, and other items of interest. During the visit, they can question their guest about what they have learned.

At higher grades, the school library can host poetry slams in cooperation with a creative writing teacher. Showcase your poetry collection for the event, and prominently display student writing. If the writing program is well developed, make sure you subscribe to magazines that publish students' work and look for websites that do the same.

Maintain a heightened awareness of other events scheduled in the school library meant to showcase student work and accomplishments. Look for ways to show how your program advances these achievements. Whenever your facility is being used for an event that brings in parents or the community, if at all possible you should be present and show how the school library contributes toward the event's success.

In the Spotlight

1. What theme can you use for a reading activity that will capture your students' interest?

2. List three things you can do to promote the SLP during a book fair.

   _____

   _____

   _____

3. What sources are available to you for finding authors and paying their fees?

4. Identify one student-related event in middle or high school where you can showcase the SLP.

Cocurricular Programs

In *New on the Job*,[1] we discussed the benefits of participating in cocurricular activities as a means of enhancing relationships with students. However, your involvement can generate additional positive results as a natural outgrowth of what you do for and with the members of the club or team. This is particularly true if you keep in mind what students want and need.

One immediate outcome of being an advisor for an activity is that its members tend to come to the school library on a more regular basis before and after school and during lunch. If you lead them well, they become strong allies with their power being amplified because the support comes from the entire group. Their acceptance and respect for you is communicated to other students, strengthening your position.

You can also draw on students' expertise. In one situation the school librarian was the advisor for the school's academic decathlon team. A significant number of the members were computer geeks with deep knowledge of operating systems and software. They helped determine how well newly installed firewalls worked, alerted the school librarian to how students circumvented the proxy server to get past filters, and shared their findings on the effectiveness of different web browsers, search engines, and related matters. By your acknowledgment of their skills and your willingness to learn from them, students feel they are being treated as adults. Parent chaperones accompanying the team to competitions express how much they appreciate what is being done for their children.

When students in the activity you advise apply for college or special scholarships and need letters of recommendation, you are in a position to show their nonacademic achievements and capabilities. When a teacher writing a recommendation minimized a student's leadership skills, an alert guidance counselor sought a counter letter from the school librarian who knew the student from a cocurricular activity. She praised him for being a role model and for providing quiet support to team members who had difficulties. Not only was the student accepted to the college of his choice, he was placed in a special honors program. The father made a point of coming to the school library to thank the school librarian in person.

As budgets cause staff cuts, harried school librarians should consider forming a library club. In line with treating students as adults, do not limit them to the drudge jobs of shelving books. Instead, give them a section, preferably in a subject in which they have an interest. Include both the circulating and reference books in this category. Encourage them to create displays from this area, read and shift shelves as needed, and suggest titles for discard.

Artistically talented students can create bulletin boards, and all of them can check books in and out. Give them first pick of new titles and seek their advice about ordering books. Have them help you make decisions on whether to keep or discontinue an online subscription. By welcoming their help on all levels, you grant them true ownership of the SLP, and they will reward you by helping you make it exemplary. When you write recommendations for them, you can address their information literacy skills.

Beyond Academics

1. In what ways do you think your students can help strengthen your SLP?
2. Which cocurricular activity is the most natural fit with the SLP?
3. How can you connect with the parents of students involved in this activity?

KEY IDEAS

- Students are your most important stakeholders, but their power comes mainly through their connection with their parents.
- Students want adults to respect and care about them.
- Students want adults to be fair and treat them all equally whether they are at the top or the bottom of their class.
- Acting out is frequently caused by anger at being regarded as not having much potential for success.
- Rules should be stated positively and should be assessed to ensure they are not counterproductive.
- Students like structure and the sense that the adult is confidently in charge of the situation.
- Lessons should have a beginning, middle, and end that flow seamlessly from one segment to the next.
- To minimize misbehavior, your furniture and layout should be age appropriate.
- Introduce literature-based research projects in grades 1 and 2.
- Incorporate storytime when working with intermediate students to continue developing their love of reading.
- Middle schoolers have the most challenging physical and emotional disparities even at the same grade level.
- Recognize the signs of bullying and be prepared to implement school policies.
- Treating middle school students as "almost adults" and being ready to learn from *them* is the best way to have them listen to you.
- By your actions, always show middle school students that you like working with this age group.
- Students move into full adolescence in high school.
- High school students want to be treated as adults, even if their behavior shows they are not there yet.

- Juniors and seniors have their eye on their future whether it is college, the military, or the workforce.
- Managing the environment of the school library is challenging particularly when lunch and classes overlap. Have students help in developing procedures to be followed.
- High school students believe they know everything about research. Have them begin their assignment without any instruction, then gather them back to assess how successful their approaches are.
- Sponsoring special events and advising cocurricular activities not only promote the objectives of the SLP but also show parents what a valuable asset it is to their children's success.

Note

1. R. Toor and H. K. Weisburg, *New on the Job: A School Library Media Specialist's Guide to Success* (Chicago: American Library Association, 2007), 76–77.

PART III
Thinking Bigger

Until now, our focus has been on developing your leadership and advocacy skills so that you are a visible, vital presence in your building. However, just as it was necessary for you to emerge from the school library in order to be successful, it is equally important for you to take an active role on a larger stage. Too often, what happens in your district is the result of pressures and issues from the outside. What happens in your state capital and in Washington, D.C., frequently has a direct impact on you and your job.

It is not enough to develop partnerships only locally. You need to move into a broader arena. Once again, you are likely to feel that you already have too much to do and certainly do not have the time—and sometimes the energy—to deal with state and national issues. Realistically, you do not have much choice. These larger challenges are likely to overwhelm much of what you have achieved unless you are prepared to act.

Before throwing up your hands in despair, look at some of the benefits. When you participate in the state and national scene, you become more adept at managing people and crises at the local level. The skills you polish in your district make you more effective on the bigger stage. In addition, you attract more allies and supporters, easing the workload. Of course, you are never operating alone when you deal with state and national issues.

Knowing of potential legislative actions early in the game helps you prepare for them on the district level. Your ability to forewarn administrators who may not be as aware as you are also increases your value to them. Using the skills you have acquired, you can work with them to develop a positive response to new directives—ones that will secure your position and the place of the SLP in the educational community.

To make an ongoing impact in the minds of stakeholders, you need to utilize the power of story and learn to combine public relations, marketing, and advocacy into a powerful force. Lessons learned from politicians come in handy as you recognize the importance of having a clear, simple message—and not letting anyone cause you to deviate from it. Subtle, nonverbal messages need to work *for* you, not against you. The first step is to discover what signals you are sending and make corrections as necessary.

Because what happens in your district most often has its roots well beyond it, you need to get involved not only at the state level but with national library organizations as well. You must join at least one. Many well-known leaders participate in two or more of the ones discussed.

Although it sometimes seems that getting support is an uphill fight that you are not going to win, you can make it happen, as two highly successful state-level advocacy campaigns demonstrate. Both suggest methods that can be adapted to meet the specific situation in your state. You might, at some point, contact the principal players directly for advice. One of the amazing things to learn is that these people are passionate about their cause and very willing to share their knowledge, particularly when it comes to saving school libraries.

From the beginning, this book has been more than a guide to surviving in difficult times. The idea is for the SLP to be valued and to thrive, recognized as a vital contributor to student success in *all* economic climates—no matter what happens with technology or new administrators or changes in curriculum. Although there are no guarantees in life, you can be sure that you ignore advocacy at your own risk. However, you also cannot trust that everything will work out. It is important to learn to anticipate what might occur and have an exit strategy ready. Positioning yourself by showing the involvement of the SLP with partners from the business and technology worlds as well as by improving your credentials are two additional avenues to make yourself valued and vital.

Ending as we began, the last chapter concludes by turning the focus back on you. You are the visible manifestation of the SLP. You must present that image in everything you do—every day.

CHAPTER 8
How Does Advocacy Develop Leadership?

Can you answer the title query? What about reversing it? The title of this chapter is somewhat loaded, as it is more of the chicken-or-the-egg question. You cannot advocate successfully unless you are a leader. But once you become good at advocating, your leadership skills increase. Although it is difficult to determine which of the two comes first, what is required is the commitment to lead and to continue to get better at doing so.

An ongoing theme of this book is the development of tools and techniques to help you not only survive but thrive. Previous chapters have detailed how to become a visible leader so that your program will be recognized as vital to the continuing success of students. In reality, you have been simultaneously building your advocacy skills. However, in order to use this ability, you need to have a clear understanding of what advocacy involves.

ADVOCACY IN PRACTICE

Most school librarians believe that advocacy is important. What they mean by the term is that they want to promote the value of the SLP and have others support it as well. Obviously that backing is the desired end, but it fails to take into consideration what an advocacy plan entails.

Advocacy has become a complex term as people have come to recognize what is necessary in order to achieve a desired outcome. On the basic level, definitions refer to active support for a cause. However, the more sophisticated explanations recognize that advocacy involves *influencing* others. The challenge is be able to do so without appearing to be manipulative.

By now you should realize that what you say about the SLP will most often be regarded as self-interest, and, if you are not focused on what your listeners value, you will be ignored. Therefore, though your ultimate goal is to have a broad spectrum of stakeholders advocating for you, you usually need to be supporting others in their campaigns. Mutual support forms strong advocacy ties. It is a dance in which one group leads and then another. If your skills are honed, you can be the one leading most often.

First and foremost, recognize that advocacy is an ongoing, never-ending campaign. You will not be implementing it every day, but you must *always* be aware of it, ready to seize opportunities as they are presented. You also seek out occasions to make those invaluable connections and show your support for others, building up a bank of favors you can draw on when needed. However, be mindful that you do not want others perceiving that you champion their causes only in the expectation of having them rally to yours. To avoid this perception, you must truly believe in the causes you support. They should in some way connect to your vision and mission; then what you do for others will be honest—even though your program will benefit from it.

Review the strategic plan you created in chapter 3. Develop at least one goal that is tied to establishing an advocacy program. For example, you might become familiar with the goals of potential partners. Know what the International Reading Association is trying to accomplish and where it is facing challenges. Be aware of what your superintendent and principal see as major goals. What can you do to support these?

When one of your stakeholders has an issue that becomes newsworthy, consider how it affects your program and what you can do to improve the situation. In addition to the previously discussed bullying, hazing might become a cause célèbre. It might be occurring with an athletic team or an incoming class. Is an administrator or an athletic director under fire as a result? Are parents concerned and looking for solutions? You are skilled at getting accurate information. Do the research and get it to the parties who need it. Suggest a workshop. If you are not the best person to present it, offer to find someone who is.

Advocacy in Action

1. How often do you read the local newspaper?
2. Do you know the issues that concern any and all of your stakeholders?
3. Which issues are currently surfacing?
4. What can you do to support issues of your potential partners?
5. What advocacy goal are you putting into your strategic plan?

TELLING STORIES

Most school librarians are skilled at storytelling, but, as an advocate, you want others telling the tale. In his book *A Whole New Mind*, Daniel H. Pink discusses the Six Senses necessary for today's world. Two of them, Story and Symphony, are of particular importance when you create strategies for your advocacy plan.[1]

Pink notes that with all the information available, no matter what you might marshal to present a case, someone can always come up with a counterclaim. To make a lasting impression that goes beyond basic facts, you must be able to present a great story. It must be crafted to touch people and make them remember the importance of what you do for students, their education, and their future.

Along with Story is Symphony, and that is another talent that is part of the school librarian's arsenal. Symphony is about cutting across traditional lines and holding a big picture, "being able to combine disparate pieces into an arresting new whole."[2] You think this way all the time when you help students with research, connecting their topic to areas that they might not have realized are relevant.

Look for ways to tell stories that have meaning for the different audiences who are your stakeholders. Know what moves them and be creative. As you build partnerships, be attuned to the ways people thank you. When you are told something substantive, write it down and ask permission to quote the person. If possible, grab a flip camera and make a video or take a picture.

When students are busily working in the school library, take pictures or videos of them in action. "Interview" them and have them describe what they are doing and learning. Record teacher comments as well. If you have long-standing volunteers, ask them to talk about what they think of the school librarian and to include specific incidents that have helped form their opinions. Create files of these testimonials that you can draw on as needed.

Students, of course, tell the most compelling stories. You can safely use their pictures on a poster with quotations from them or even make a podcast if you are presenting these at a board of education meeting, but any type of publication, particularly on the Internet, requires consent forms. Despite these barriers, it is worth showcasing what students see themselves getting, or, even more compelling, what they feel they are losing.

An inner-city school librarian who must carry her reference resources between two schools told of having a tug-of-war with a fourth grader. The school librarian had to tear an encyclopedia volume from the girl's hands in order to get to her next school on time. The image quickly burns itself into the mind. What are the powers-that-be doing? How dare they suppress the desire to learn, hampering children already handicapped by socioeconomic conditions? And doing it in the name of fiscal prudence! This is a story that has power.

"Why I love my library" contests are a rich source of story. If your state library association runs this essay contest, make sure you get your students to enter. In places where it does not, hold one on your own in April to celebrate School Library Month. See if local businesses will offer prizes. This approach not only gets the community involved, it saves you from spending your own money.

Have a committee of teachers and parents do the judging. Their participation represents a buy-in on their part. Create a splashy awards night to honor the winners—and the business supporters. Give small gifts to all who entered. Acknowledge the help of the judges and have some tokens of appreciation for them. Create posters with excerpts from all the entrants (with their pictures if possible) and spread these around the room. Have winners read their essays. The local media will pick up the best sound bites for you.

Although you will definitely be using your stories if your job is threatened, it is far better to be proactive so that dire situations do not arise. Consider venues for bringing your stories to the attention of others. For example, with the approval of your principal, plan a display in the halls as well as the school library at a back-to-school or conference night. Invite parents to come in to see your facility. (As a lure, you can offer a prize that they can give to their child, such as an amnesty on overdue books or a coupon for free ice cream from the cafeteria.) When they arrive, have a video playing that shows classes at work in the SLP. Set up a display of materials that would be of interest to parents and permit them to borrow these.

A bigger stretch is to ask for permission to showcase the SLP to the board of education. In that situation, it is best if the presentation is done by all the school librarians in the district. Find out exactly how long you have and make sure you use a bit *less* time.

The local chamber of commerce, realtors, and other groups occasionally visit the high school and are greeted by the principal, superintendent of schools, and other administrators. Typically, the school library is used for the welcoming and closing remarks. Take this opportunity to feature your stories. Keep gathering them and looking for ways to tell them to the world.

Storytime

1. Briefly describe one great story that reveals the impact your SLP has made on a student's life.

2. What student project could be used to tell a story of the role of the SLP in student learning?

3. Which of these projects use twenty-first-century skills?

4. To which events could you bring these stories?

THREE-STEP APPROACH

Although you are now developing a better understanding of what constitutes advocacy, you also need to be aware of how it differs from public relations and marketing. You will be using all three of these tools to ensure that all stakeholders are aware of your program, know how they benefit from it, and are willing to actively support it on all fronts. We suggested this three-step approach in *New on the Job: A School Library Media Specialist's Guide to Success.*[3]

Public Relations and Promotion

Public relations (PR) is about presenting a strong, positive image of your program and having the public develop a favorable view of it. *Promotion* refers to the techniques you employ to keep that program in the public eye. Combine the two for the best results.

The opening screen of the OPAC (online public access catalog) is one highly visible means to communicate your message. Another is your website, which can be the most visible—if it is accessed regularly. Linking the two adds to the impact of both.

Most integrated library systems (ILS) or automation programs allow you to design a home page that features your library. Use any technical support that vendors are willing to give you to make it as slick and professional as possible. Although a picture that shows your facility in the best possible light is an absolute must, it is even better if you have several that scroll by or vary when the site is opened. Students researching on computers and working in groups are the strongest images, but you need to be sure that you are following district privacy guidelines.

Your OPAC opening screen can also feature recent acquisitions, student reviews, and upcoming events. Check with your vendor to find out if you can view what other schools using the system have done and select the best ideas from those. Of course, you should have a link to your website, which will promote traffic.

Suggestions about what to include on your website have been mentioned in other chapters, but do include the link to your OPAC. You might also consider one to the public library and ask them to link to your website or OPAC or both. This will get you in the eye of the general public as well as of parents, teachers, and students.

Your tagline, which you created in chapter 1, should be present on your OPAC and website. If you have any supply funds or petty cash (or are willing to invest some of your own money), have pencils or pens imprinted with that tagline. Hand them to parents or teachers when you do a presentation. Any time you create a bibliography (print or online or brochure), be sure to include your tagline. Both the product and the brief message serve to give you that strong public image and promote your program.

School Library Month is a perfect opportunity for public relations and promotions. The American Association of School Librarians offers myriad activities and ideas prepackaged for you to use. You can download public service announcements (PSAs) and other resources that are ready to use and that allow you to fill in your school information (and tagline). Each year has a brand-new collection of materials, and you can also access the archives starting with 2008. Go to www.aasl.org and search on School Library Month. The archives are a link at the left side of the page.

Although you may do a number of different public relations activities throughout the year or repeat one (such as pencils with the tagline), PR is mostly a series of quick reminders that keep your program front and center. It is meant to prevent you from disappearing from view. Compared with marketing and advocacy, public relations and promotion are the shortest term. You can do them quickly as long as you have a stockpile of ideas. Do check the AASL website and that of your state organization, so you do not need to create these activities on your own. Share your best ideas with others, and have them do the same for you.

Front and Center

1. What PR and promotion techniques have you used so far?

2. Which were most successful? What made them so?

3. How would you rate your OPAC as a PR tool?

4. What can you do to make it better?

5. How much traffic does your website get? What will you do to improve your site?

6. Where are some places you can add your tagline?

7. What will you do for School Library Month?

Marketing

The term *marketing* historically refers to moving goods from the producer into the hands of the consumer, with an exchange of money. Obviously that is not what is meant when marketing the SLP is discussed. In this context, you want to "sell" your product to a specific audience.

To reach your target, you need a plan. Planning takes time and thought, and you have little to spare with your daily responsibilities. Fortunately you created a strategic plan in chapter 3, and your marketing plan should fit within it. As an illustration, a suggested goal was to collaborate with three teachers on an animal unit. These were teachers with whom you had never worked before. How can you reach them and sell your program and services to them?

The first step is to make them aware you exist. Sure, they know there is a school library and that you head it, but they still haven't made the connection between it and what they do. That is now your job. Invite them to your facility before or after school as individuals or all together, whatever works best. Let them know you are providing food, suggesting a friendly, informal gathering. Make sure you maintain that atmosphere throughout. You might even learn what their personal interests and hobbies are at this time. Being able to connect personally with teachers increases the likelihood of collaboration. Also, if you know some things about them, you can send them books, websites, and the like, on topics they care about.

Select the best and most helpful animal books from your collection, including any reference sets. Have your computers open to any databases you have available as well as one or two good websites. Let them know you are just sharing with them the resources they can draw on. As they munch away and flip through books or explore the online materials, note their reactions. Are they developing an interest in what you have?

Answer any questions they have, but do not push further. The old axiom is "No one wants to be sold, but everyone wants to buy." These teachers have been resisting, avoiding, or simply overlooking your existence. You do not want to pressure them; they will just retreat. Thank them for coming.

Follow up with a message. E-mail is fine, but in this day and age a handwritten note can be even better. Again, thank them for giving up their time to join you in the school library. Let them know you would love to help them out when they teach their animal unit. Suggest that you can create a bibliography including websites for them, for their students, or for both. You want to build their desire to work with you. Pull back if you feel resistance, but return a while later with something a bit smaller, such as a particularly good website.

When you get a response from them, you know you have made the necessary connection. Now you want to produce an action together. Find out their plans for the unit. Suggest areas where you can contribute, whether it is direct teaching or working with students when the class comes to the school library. (You might not get full collaboration the first time.) If the project is not inquiry-based or does not have students using twenty-first-century skills, carefully offer some ideas to add to the assignment that will incorporate aspects of critical thinking, information literacy, ethical uses of information, and other abilities that students will need to succeed. If you are the one responsible for these aspects, your recommendations are likely to be accepted.

You can get help with marketing the SLP from the AASL version of the ALA Campaign for America's Libraries. Click on "Issues and Advocacy" on the AASL home page (www.aasl.org) and select "@ your library® School Library Campaign." The toolkit is downloadable in Word or as a pdf file and has a wealth of suggestions.

Although public relations is of short duration, marketing takes longer. It tends to be focused on a specific audience so that you can tailor the message to the recipient. Because you are expending your very precious time, you must make sure you are going to get results. Build in places where you will assess how well you are proceeding to your goal. Make adjustments as needed. You will get better at it the more you do it.

In the Marketplace

1. Who will be your target audience?
2. What will you do to raise awareness?
3. How can you stimulate an interest in what your program can offer?
4. What will be the hook that will encourage your target to want to use your services?
5. How can you check to be sure you are on course for success?

Adding Advocacy

Complete the three-step approach with advocacy, the motivating factor behind your public relations and marketing efforts. You have created a strong, positive image of your program, hopefully outside the school as well as within it. You targeted a specific audience to work with you; now you need to have them ready to be your champion.

Although the new *Empowering Learners: Guidelines for School Library Media Programs*[4] has superseded *Information Power: Building Partnerships for Learning,*[5] the old subtitle is a reminder of what you must always keep uppermost in your mind. Advocacy is about building partnerships. The process is never-ending because you cannot develop a relationship and then leave it alone without repercussions.

You must also be constantly on the lookout for other places where you should be making that relationship connection. What makes advocacy so challenging is that you usually create ties to people based on their positions. For example, you know teachers, board members, administrators, and the president of the home-school association. However, people leave and are replaced by others. Unless the partnership was institutionalized in some way—such as a position statement on the website of the parent organization—you have to start all over again with the new person.

Many a school librarian has discovered that when a principal or superintendent left, she took with her the history of the contributions the SLP had made to the educational community. The new administrator arrived with preconceived notions of the value of the school librarian based on his previous experience. A little research is sometimes necessary to learn something about this principal or superintendent in his former job. Was he a strong supporter of SLPs? Did the school librarians have a good relationship with him? What is his particular strength? Is he tech-savvy or tech-phobic? Wise school librarians plan public relations activities and a marketing strategy as soon as the new hire is announced. Once they have achieved a base level of recognition, they move in with a subtext of "How can I help you?" If they have done their research well, they will also have some concrete suggestions.

Obviously, as much as possible you should be striving to have your various partners acknowledge your program within their individual groups. One state library association had its PTA pass a resolution in support of SLPs. Although this was a great start, it had to be followed up with regular reinforcements, such as having a school librarian corner on the PTA's site. There, parents can ask questions or get advice on literature, and information literacy that is relevant and of value to them can be disseminated.

If you have successfully reached those teachers you targeted in your marketing strategy, suggest you put on a program at *their* conference, showcasing the value of collaboration. This achieves several positive results. The teacher will be acknowledged within the school (or district or both), leading to further connections with you. You demonstrate to other teachers in that subject area what the possibilities are for them in their school—and build a base of support that extends beyond your building. And, you make your other teachers consider that working with you can benefit them.

At all times you want to be aware of who the power wielders are. A board of education member may have more sway than the board president. An assistant superintendent with an agenda can line up supporters and have an impact greater than that of the superintendent. You will never win everyone to your camp, but you want your logical allies to be strongly advocating for you. The flip is to minimize the impact of those who might work against you by either having very strong forces in your corner or finding ways to keep your opposition from becoming too insistent. The latter is more difficult; it requires an understanding of what motivates your opponents and then showing that the SLP will not be an impediment.

Always Advocating

1. Who are your partners?

2. Are your partnerships institutionalized or completely based on the person?

3. What can you do to become embedded in the agenda and programs of others?

4. Pretend your current principal was just arriving on the job.

    What would you want to know in advance?

    What would your marketing strategy be?

    What could you do to "help"?

STAYING ON MESSAGE

Learn from the politicians. Their handlers know the importance of staying on message—which means not getting drawn into discussing anything that is off the points you are striving to make. You do not want to muddy the waters and risk being misquoted or taken out of context.

Know what your messages are. You should have a list that is virtually committed to memory. Some are taglines such as "All kids succeed @ the library." Others are basic statements such as "Research has shown that students in schools with active SLPs, staffed by certificated school librarians, score higher on high-stakes tests." You might want to stress the economic importance of your program by focusing on this: "The SLP is designed to make students high achievers in the global economy." Be familiar with what AASL and your state association are saying about the role of the SLP and then choose the one(s) with the most resonance for your particular audience.

Once you have your messages (not too many), you need to know how to focus on them. One of the biggest errors you can make is going into a defensive posture. For example, if a district faced with budget cuts is planning to eliminate many school librarians, someone is bound to ask you whether you consider school librarians to be more important than teachers. What are the dangers inherent in this question, and how can you respond without creating new problems?

Although you cannot agree that teachers are more important—or you have just defeated your position—you must also *never* deny a question posed that way. Denial only reinforces the statement. So you must not say, "I don't think we are more important than teachers, but . . . ." What will be heard is that sentence without the negative. Now you are in trouble with teachers, and you need their support as well. Remember that any time you make a negative comment about teachers or even about administrators, you are opening up the likelihood of being tarred with the same brush. As far as the general public is concerned, we are a single entity. If you point out failings, it is assumed that these relate to your program as well.

If you pay attention to how politicians answer the "gotcha" questions, you know the focus must stay on your message. Say something like, "The first priority of the SLP is student success, not only on high-stakes tests but in the global marketplace that they will be entering." Then go on to explain why the SLP is uniquely positioned to deliver on that commitment.

Another related lesson from politics is to always speak from the position of a winner. No one wants to support a loser. There is nothing to gain from it. When a candidate who is far behind in the polls is interviewed, invariably the response is, "We are seeing an upsurge and our crowds are increasing at our rallies." The candidate will then immediately recite a *story* of one voter who spoke about an issue dear to the theme of the campaign. In so doing, the message is reinforced, and listeners feel that here is an underdog with a chance of scoring a big upset.

Speaking from scarcity is not compelling. It turns people off. It does not matter if you are right. If you whine, you will not get heard. You may hear expressions of sympathy, but they will not translate into anything meaningful. Although Americans love underdogs, they only stay with them if they are going to win. You want to be seen as a fighter for a good cause that you want *them* to join.

Your Message Is Important

1. List your three top messages.

   _____

   _____

   _____

2. How would you respond to the question "Aren't school libraries unnecessary in the age of the Internet?"

3. How can you discuss shrinking budget dollars for the SLP without whining?

NONVERBAL MESSAGES

Staying on message goes beyond knowing what to say and when. No matter how good your communication skills are, you can be strengthened or damaged by the nonverbal messages you and your facility send. It is a truism that we teach people how to treat us. What is surprising is that external clues can affect the decisions people make about how to do so. More often than not, their initial reaction is based on how you dress, your demeanor, and even how you move, often without their being aware of it. Even if you are astute enough to recognize this assessment, it can take a long time and much hard work on your part to cause people to change their first impression.

Do you look like a professional or a stereotypical "librarian"? You can argue that you get down on the floor with students at times or that there is no dress code for faculty. The fact is, however, if you look like an administrator, you are more likely to be treated as one. If your personal style is frumpy, you are apt to be dismissed as someone of little importance.

You need not wear skirts or dresses if you are a woman or a suit if you are a man. Men may also wear clean, well-fitting blue jeans if accompanied by a shirt (not a T-shirt) and a blazer or sweater. Women's pants can be stylish and still allow for needed movement. Sneakers are not appropriate unless it is a field day. Your wardrobe should include *good-looking,* comfortable shoes. Low heels for women are better than flats. Yes, you are on your feet a lot, but there are many brands that will not cause aching arches at the end of the day. If you are ever at a large state or national conference, check the shoes worn by the exhibitors. Women invariably wear heels, and men are *not* in sneakers. You do not have to check badges to see who the vendors are and who the librarians are.

Body language also communicates information. Your attitude is translated into your posture, which people read without thinking about it. If you are feeling misunderstood, unappreciated, and undervalued, it affects your demeanor. If you think you are a fabulous school librarian with the best job in the building, you will walk and talk completely differently. The ability of internal reactions to control outward appearances and affect the perceptions of others is at the core of the affirmations some consider silly. These positive assertions do not have the inherent magic ascribed to them by those who repeat them daily. What they do is help you focus on a strong self-image, which you then project without conscious thought. The result is that the people you come in contact with will react positively to you.

Your speech also affects the way you are treated. Are your sentences punctuated with frequent hesitations (e.g., "um" or "uh")? These interjections suggest uncertainty and a lack of confidence. Do you often say "you know" or "actually" or other repetitive phrases that mean nothing in conversation? These diminish the power of your message. Have you succumbed to that annoying intonation pattern that goes up at the end of a declarative sentence as if it were a question? This, too, implies that you are not sure of what you are saying. Pay attention to these subtle messages from others. Listen as teachers speak and note how many have these speech habits. Consider how much more effective they would sound if they could eliminate these. Then work on clearing up any that you have.

Louder Than Words

1. How professional is your wardrobe?

2. What could you do to upgrade it?

3. List two mental attitudes that will help you feel powerful as you go through your day.

_____

_____

4. What speech patterns or habits do you need to change?

ROOM WITH A VIEW

The school library is your office, your classroom, and your home. As such it represents your philosophy, mission, and vision to everyone who enters, while you are there or after school hours. *New on the Job* had you assess your facility to determine whether it was student-friendly and welcoming in general; however, it is also a vehicle that can promote or detract from your message.[6]

How does your school library show that it is an exciting, vibrant place even when no one is present? For too many busy school librarians, the chief indication is a desk piled high with papers, books, and mail. It is hard to get to everything when you have so much to do each day. However, when parents and others are in the school library for a meeting, they see your mess and decide you are disorganized or sloppy or both. Although you can justifiably argue that such a judgment is unfair and unrealistic, their perception is what it is.

Purchase storage tubs of different sizes, hot files, and other office storage paraphernalia. Take ten minutes before you leave to sweep the day's detritus into cabinets and bins and whatever else you have acquired to get the mess out of sight. This cleanup will help you as well when you come back in the morning. Facing a desk piled high is a depressing way to begin the day. After a while, you will have a system worked out, and these resources will help keep you focused on your current task without the distraction of nonrelated papers.

Look around your room as though you were entering it as a guest. Does it say this is where twenty-first-century learning takes place? Or is the space mired somewhere in the 1980s or 1990s? Card catalogs, used or not, are antiques. Earth-tone color schemes are outdated. Somehow, you must update the look and bring in bold colors and furniture appropriate for students and today's learning. Consider the age and physical needs of your students. If you are in a K–5 school, you need tables and chairs of different heights to accommodate everyone. Tables should be on casters so they can be easily moved to new configurations. In the upper grades you should have laptop-friendly spaces. Chairs are not always the best seating for every purpose at all levels. For elementary story sessions or even for students looking through books, you may want benches or floor cushions. Middle and high school students appreciate a café atmosphere with high-top tables. Oddly enough, 1950s-style, diner-type booths are big favorites with teens in a lounge area.

If the look of your school library is not twenty-first century, visitors and patrons will think your program is no different from what it was twenty years ago. Look around your room and determine what has to go and what needs to be added. Do the research and find out what the changes will cost. Start a committee to help with the planning. Include students, teachers, and parents if possible. Students are your end users, so what they want is paramount, but you want the input from others as well.

Furniture is not cheap, but there is a large price range. If the budget dollars are not there (and they rarely are), you will have to find another way. Fundraising, gifts from graduating classes (or from an active alumni association), contributions from the parent association, or a grant from the local education foundation are all possible sources. Local businesses might make in-kind donations as well as contribute to the costs. Your advocacy skills are invaluable here.

Figure out the project you want to do. Have several levels to ensure that you can make some changes. Get your administrators on board first, and let your remodeled school library tell the world that it is the gateway to twenty-first-century learning.

Speaking Volumes

1. Is your office ready for company?

2. What immediate steps can you take to improve its look?

3. Check library furniture catalogs and create a wish list of purchases to update the school library. What are your first choices?

4. Who will be on your remodeling committee?

5. Where can you go to get the funds you will need?

KEY IDEAS

- Advocacy and leadership are two sides of the same coin. You cannot do one without the other.
- Effective advocates know how to influence others to become active supporters without being manipulative.
- To be successful, advocacy must be continually present in your awareness and planning.
- Be on the lookout for stories that bring compelling life to the value of your program.
- Select the right one among these stories to bring to a specific group of stakeholders.
- Know how to present a positive image of your role and program to the school and community.
- Incorporate the elements of a marketing plan into your strategic planning.
- Focus on building partnerships to create a strong base of supporters.
- Identify your main messages and avoid responding to distractions that will lessen their impact.
- Your dress and attitude send messages about you and your program.
- Speech patterns can suggest that you are not confident in your proposals and actions.

Notes

1. Daniel H. Pink, *A Whole New Mind: Why Right-Brainers Will Rule the Future* (New York: Riverhead Books, 2006), 65–66.
2. Ibid., 66.
3. R. Toor and H. K. Weisburg, *New on the Job: A School Library Media Specialist's Guide to Success* (Chicago: American Library Association, 2007), 76–77.
4. American Association of School Librarians, *Empowering Learners: Guidelines for School Library Media Programs* (Chicago: AASL, 2009).
5. ALA/AECT, *Information Power: Building Partnerships for Learning* (Chicago: American Library Association, 1998).
6. Toor and Weisburg, *New on the Job*, 57–59.

CHAPTER 9
How Do You Get a Larger Perspective?

If I fly high, I will get to see much more!

Before turning to the title query, another question should be answered first. Why do you need a larger perspective? By now you recognize that the SLP does not exist in a vacuum. It is a component of the school and district educational program, which in turn is part of the community that funds it. Doing an outstanding job in the school library will benefit your students, but if no one knows what you are doing, your program is likely to be cut or eliminated.

In the same vein, the school district is part of a larger whole, affected by economic and political realities that shape its choices and decisions. You need to become aware of these forces, know what is happening in other locations, and learn what resources are available to you beyond your local situation. In other words, you must step even farther outside your comfort zone to make time to participate on a bigger scale.

AT THE STATE LEVEL

If you have not yet done so, you must join your state association. Depending on your location, school librarians will either be a section within the larger library organization or be independent. For example, the school librarians in New York are part of the New York Library Association (NYLA), while the New Jersey Association of School Librarians (NJASL) is separate from the New Jersey Library Association (NJLA), but the two have cordial relations. Find the website for the state association that represents you and become a member.

Membership should be more than paying dues. If you want to get the most out of your association, you have to participate. Start by exploring the website. Note what events are being scheduled and what resources are provided. Plan on attending the next conference held by your association. (In some states where the organization is not strong, you might want to see what neighboring states offer.)

In many places, getting released time to attend these meetings is difficult. Look over the program (usually it is posted online) and note which sessions would be most relevant to you. Discuss with your principal or supervisor what you plan to do with the knowledge you expect to gain. Will you be able to conduct a workshop for teachers? Will you be looking at a new way to improve student achievement? Suggest that seeing the exhibits will give you a chance to better evaluate databases and other materials so that the school will get the most benefit from any budget dollars expended. Be prepared to take personal time if you are not given a professional day. Although this requirement may seem unfair, realize your attendance will strengthen your leadership skills and ensure that you are a visible, vital presence in your building.

Consider submitting a proposal to do a presentation at the next conference. Being on the program strengthens your request for a professional day. It also adds to your visibility and credibility within your school. Find time afterward to share with your principal or supervisor the reactions from the attendees. You might even be able to repeat your presentation for your teachers (if it is appropriate) or the other school librarians in the district at the next staff development day.

Make time to become familiar with your association's website. Learn who the officers and chairs of the different committees are. Look for a committee that is a good fit with your interests and volunteer to serve on it. Working with your colleagues on the state level widens your appreciation and understanding of what is happening in other districts. You may discover that some of the challenges you are facing have already been resolved by others and that their solutions can be adapted to fit your situation.

Talking about what is happening in your district will bring your issues to the attention of the state leadership. Very often this disclosure helps to identify an emerging trend, and the state association can take action before the problem becomes too large or widespread. You are now acting on a much larger stage as you work with colleagues to build state-level partnerships to promote SLPs.

After you have had experience with committee participation, you will be ready to run for office, perhaps president. In that position your abilities to think and act from a larger perspective become second nature. Your conversations with your principal, teachers, and others will reflect your new awareness, and you will find that these stakeholders instinctively react to you as a valuable leader.

In Touch in State

1. What resources and information are available at your state association's website?

2. What committee(s) in your state organization interest you?

3. Is there a unit or activity that you could share with colleagues as a presentation at the next conference?

AT THE NATIONAL LEVEL

Once you have stretched your leadership—and advocacy—muscles at the state level, it is time to move on to the national scene. If you were elected to the presidency of your state association, you might have some ex officio role in a national organization. For example, most affiliate presidents are one of two delegates to the Affiliate Assembly of the American Association of School Librarians (AASL). Even if you have not attained that office, serving in a national organization is fifty times more powerful than at the state level because you now view the profession from Alaska to Florida and Maine to Hawaii—and can draw on the expertise of your colleagues from around the country.

If you are not yet a member, explore the websites of the three national associations. Find out where they overlap and how they are unique. For AASL, go to both www.ala.org and www.aasl.org. The website for the Association for Educational Communications and Technology (AECT) is www.aect.org, but also check http://aect-smt.org.

AECT encompasses educators and others focused on using technology to improve learning and has twenty-four state affiliates and nearly two thousand members. Its School Media and Technology Division is for school librarians and technology and communications professionals in K–12 schools. The membership fee ($99 at the time of this writing) includes divisional membership (see www.aect.org).

Similar to AECT, the International Society for Technology in Education (ISTE) represents "educators and education leaders engaged in improving learning and teaching by advancing the effective use of technology in PK–12 and higher education" (www.iste.org). The society's website lists fifty-six corporate partners from technology, communications, and education fields. Standard ISTE membership is $92 per year, including as many special interest groups (SIGs) as you care to join. Currently there are twenty of these, including media specialists.

AASL, a division within the American Library Association (ALA), is the largest by far of the national organizations for school librarians (about nine thousand members). Its mission is "to advocate excellence, facilitate change, and develop leaders in the school library media field" (www.aasl.org). Although the other two associations have technology as their driving purpose, AASL incorporates technology into the overall role of the school librarian and the SLP. Dues are higher than for AECT or ISTE ($180 for ALA/AASL personal membership; $115 the first year), but you have the benefit of being part of a huge organization that has a strong presence in Washington, D.C., and a well-established reputation as *the* organization for all librarians.

The first of AASL's essential functions is "Outreach to the Field," and in that capacity it has created the *Standards for the 21st-Century Learner*. ISTE has produced the National Educational Technology Standards for Students (NETS-S) as well as standards for teachers (NETS-T) and administrators (NETS-A). Important as these standards are, they differ from the AASL Standards both in depth and in overall focus. AASL also supports issues of concern to members and nonmembers alike, including funding, intellectual freedom, reading, and technology.[1]

To begin developing this larger view of the profession and current issues, read the blogs from these organizations. Once you are a member you can get involved very easily. Join either or both of AASL's electronic discussion lists (AASLForum and InfoLit) or the divisional electronic discussion lists at AECT. You can participate in communications from ISTE's SIGs and explore the presence of all three in Second Life. (You can also check them out on Facebook or Twitter.) These contacts will expand your awareness, but there are many more possibilities.

Even if your state has its own large conference, attending one at the national level is eye-opening. You get to see vendors who may never have come to your state but have a product that could make a difference to your program. Presentations tend to be more sophisticated, frequently from leaders in the field, and give you new ideas—and contacts—that will be invaluable. If the cost of attending seems prohibitive, check out the travel grant opportunities or become a virtual attendee. Although the latter is not quite as good as being there in person, you will still connect to what is happening nationally.

Committee membership is the next step. Very often, this involvement can get you released from your school to attend a conference, although these days you can serve virtually as well. Working with colleagues from across the country increases your understanding of what is happening nationally, clues you in to what might occur in your state and district, informs you of solutions that have been tried and any that have proved successful, and, on a very personal level, provides a network of knowledgeable friends willing to assist you when you need help.

Seeking national office is the ultimate participation at this level, but, even if you are not prepared to do so, your involvement will bring you benefits on a daily basis. Your new expertise will show in your conversations with administrators and teachers. The confidence you gain from being recognized by other school librarians will be reflected in your demeanor and speech, and you will be sending the nonverbal messages that earn you the respect of others. Your leadership becomes evident, and what you say and advocate for are taken seriously.

A National Voice

1. Based on your investigation, which of the national organizations will you join?

2. If you already belong to a national organization, what other one are you considering?

3. What will be your first step in being an active, participating member?

4. How will you let your administrators know about your involvement?

POLITICALLY SPEAKING

Gone are the days when your interest in politics was solely a personal choice. In today's world what happens in government directly affects how you do your job and, sometimes, whether or not you have one. Your awareness begins at the local level but must proceed all the way to the federal government.

In chapter 5, the one element of the community that was not discussed was the government. The differences among schools in a large city, a suburban town, and a rural community are huge. In the latter two, mayors (or the equivalent) rarely serve full time. Frequently, they work locally and can be seen in their place of business. Their children might be in your school. Where the population is low, everyone knows one another. By contrast, in big cities the mayor tends to be extremely powerful and has at least some authority over the board of education and the head of the school system.

In smaller locations, it is a simple matter to invite the mayor or members of the local government or both to your school library for a program in which they might read to students at the elementary level or participate on a panel with Q&A from a middle or high school student audience. To achieve a similar result in the larger political structures, you have to go through layers of government personnel and deal with a crowded calendar. You will not get on it unless it is to the political advantage of the mayor or you have some special "carrot" to offer. (For example, you might have won a large grant and are presenting it to parents and others. In this case, it becomes an opportunity for the mayor to promote his or her education agenda.)

No matter the size of your district, look for ways to have these politicians visit your school library, see its potential, and become a supporter. Sometimes, the first step is to work with the other school librarians to create the proper venue to attract them, but the publicity that ensues is good for your program and builds your connection to those who can affect the allocation of budget dollars to the schools.

Real power over your future rests heavily at the state level. For example, are school librarians mandated? If they are, it will be difficult for the local school board to eliminate your position. Many school librarians found their jobs were in jeopardy when the No Child Left Behind (NCLB) Act required schools to be staffed by "highly qualified" teachers. It was left to the states to define what was meant by that phrase. Although the education unions such as the National Education Association (NEA) fought against the label itself, school librarians in many places were in the strange position of trying to be recognized as highly qualified. In states where school librarians were not among the subject areas requiring this appellation, their districts were eliminating them.

Even more than administrators who at least come in contact at some point in their professional careers with school librarians, legislators often have no concept that the SLP has evolved and changed in the last thirty-plus years. Their mental image is rooted in the days when they were in school. Fortunately, most state library associations have a legislative committee and some sort of government relations consultant to keep abreast of what is happening and move in rapidly when an important issue is at stake.

If politics has an attraction for you, consider joining the legislative committee. No matter what, be on the alert for any messages to contact your own state legislator to urge action on an upcoming bill. Do not leave it for others to do. Numbers count here. Many states organize a Legislative Day when school, public, and academic librarians visit the state capital and meet with their respective legislators. Attendees (and it's great if you can get parents or students or both to come along) are well prepared by the legislative committee with talking points and the voting history of the person(s) they will be seeing.

ALA has a National Library Legislative Day during the first week in May. Its Washington Office works hard to ensure that all attendees are fully prepared, spending the day before the meetings briefing everyone in what they need to know and offering talking points. Again, parents and students can be the best people to present the case for school (and all) libraries. You (and they) need not travel to Washington, D.C., as you can make an impact virtually.

Whether or not you participate in "Leg Day," check the ALA Washington Office website regularly. You can quickly see the latest issues impacting libraries. The site offers many ways for you to participate, including "Issues and Advocacy."[2]

Be prepared to respond to alerts when bills are pending. You will be directed to a capwiz site that allows you to e-mail or fax your senators and representatives. When you enter your zip code, your legislators' names are displayed, and you can proceed to send the message suggested or, better yet, add your personal perspective. One click and your message is sent. The process takes a minimal amount of time, and the impact of numbers means you are likely to have influenced the legislation that will affect you and other librarians.

National politics has local effects. ALA has worked with AASL to get school librarians listed as instructional rather than support personnel. (Support staff are more likely to be eliminated in times of tight budgets.) The Washington Office has been instrumental in bringing the Strengthening Kids' Interest in Learning and Libraries (SKILLs) Act to the floor of the House, staying with it even when it was taken off the calendar. As the act "is intended to ensure that all students will have the support and resources they need for a quality education by establishing a goal that all public school libraries employ no less than one highly qualified school library media specialist,"[3] its importance to all school librarians is obvious.

Whether you become an active legislation committee member is a personal choice, but you *must* keep current with events on the political scene at all levels. Your future and that of your colleagues depends on it.

Entering the Political Arena

1. How could you bring your mayor or other local government officials to your school library?

2. What is your state association doing to make the legislature aware of the role of school librarians and the importance of SLPs?

3. How will you participate during "Leg Day"? Which parents or students or both might like to be involved?

4. What helpful information did you find on the website of the ALA Washington Office?

SUCCESSFUL CAMPAIGNS

When you are struggling to gain the recognition your program deserves, it is difficult to believe that you can have more than a symbolic victory if a crisis reaches your community. You might think the best you can hope for is some support and sympathetic words from the powers that be about how much they appreciate school libraries, but ultimately the cuts are made and the program is eliminated or so depleted of funds it cannot survive as a vital part of the school.

Although not every story is known, two notable successes are strong indications that you can win and prove your worth. Note that when the challenge goes beyond the local community, the state association needs to play a pivotal role. If you follow up these stories to get more information, you will also learn that the people involved always made sure their message was positive. They did not attack anyone. With advocacy, you need all the friends you can get. You do not want to alienate any group.

Washington Moms

In 2007 three mothers in Spokane, Washington, sat around a kitchen table, concerned by the proposal to slash hours of the school librarians. Lisa Layera Brunkan had been volunteering in her daughter's elementary school library and knew firsthand the benefits a certified school librarian brought to students. Along with her friends Susan McBurney and Denette Hill, she became an activist, testifying before the board of directors of the Spokane Public Schools and building a grassroots advocacy organization.[4]

The three moms soon drew on research from leaders in school librarianship, including Mike Eisenberg, Gary Hartzell, and Keith Curry Lance, who gave them the information they needed. Meanwhile the three started a petition drive and were supported by local newspapers and their state senator, along with the many citizens who appeared before the school board. Despite this, the board instituted the cuts. But the story does not end there.

The trio discovered that the problem was not local but statewide. Concerned at the inequity of some students getting twenty-first-century skills while others did not, the moms went back to the fray, with a promise that it would not be a "blame game." With the help of the Washington Library Media Association, Craigslist, and media outlets, they began to spread the word once more. Their website (now defunct), which included a blog and testimonials, became their strongest mobilizing force.

The group's timing was perfect, as the state legislature had just created a task force to identify lacks within the basic education program. Although the process is normally lengthy, the group was able to get a supplemental budget passed. The fact that they were moms and not lobbyists added to their effectiveness, but what mattered most was their commitment and the expertise they picked up as they went along. Businesspeople joined them, as did the mayor of Spokane. AASL and ALA sent representatives.

The Senate voted 49–0 to fund libraries statewide, but the bill was defeated in the House. One month later a compromise was worked out, and a line item of $4 million was approved for the 2008–2009 school year. The three moms continue to speak out in support of school libraries. The campaign became a model for others. There is now a Fund Our Future Oregon and another in Arizona. Encourage parents in your district to learn their story (www.schoollibraryjournal.com/article/CA6590045.html), and perhaps they will also become grassroots activists.

Cultivating the Grassroots

1. For what would you want your "moms" to campaign at the local level? At the state level?
2. What state legislators are most likely to listen to "moms" or to you on school library issues?

Ohio Plan

The Ohio Educational Library Media Association (OELMA) learned in 2000 that the state was once again reducing requirements for school librarians that would go into effect in 2002. Immediately, the OELMA leadership swung into action to create an advocacy strategy. The timeline for what occurred is summarized here. However, the specific events should not overshadow the embedded advocacy strategy that was essential to the group's eventual success. The association has a long history of advocacy and has a legislative advisor to alert the leadership to any legislative issues likely to impact school libraries. Despite these efforts, a far more intensive reaction was needed to respond to the challenge.

OELMA had a long-standing relationship with INFOhio (the information network for Ohio schools), the state library, and the state department of education. All four formed a core strategy group—Ohio's Leadership 4 School Libraries (L4SL)—which led the way. OELMA steered the work of Dr. Ross Todd and his Ohio Research Study and developed an Evidence-based Practice Training Module. The goal was to create a school librarian presence within the educational community and never again be surprised by a state action (see www.oelma.org/Ohio.htm).

In 2001 a staffing survey was begun as OELMA worked for legislation to get professional school librarians in schools (this did not occur), and the following year the Ohio Research Study got under way. By 2003 OELMA created a video on school libraries, which it mailed to every school district in the state, and an unexpected partnership with ILILE (Institute for Library and Information Literacy Education) was developed. ILILE sponsored teacher-librarian teams at the OELMA conference where Dr. Todd presented the preliminary findings of his study.

The following year, OELMA sent its advocacy chair to National Library Legislative Day to bring to the attention of Ohio's national representatives information from the Ohio Research Study, and in 2005, a congressman delivered the keynote speech at the association's annual conference. The same year, OELMA began workshops on Evidence-based Practice, training trainers to speed the process. The module, TRAILS (Tool for Real Time Assessment of Information Literacy Skills), became available in 2006.

The OELMA president sent a letter to the new governor in 2007, stressing the important role played by school librarians in student learning. The same year, representatives met with the Partnership for 21st Century Skills and attended various board of education meetings. By 2008, OELMA had a delegate at the Governor's Institute on Creativity and Innovation in Education, and members were sent to different locations where the governor was holding public meetings on education. In addition, INFOhio published a white paper entitled "Preparing 21st Century Ohio Learners for Success."[5]

In 2009, all the work of OELMA paid off. A bill was introduced with language detailing twenty-first-century student literacies (media and information literacy were included). OELMA and its advocacy committee prepared testimony for House Finance Committee hearings to adjust the wording of the bill so that it would specify licensed librarians and media specialists. By spring, a list of talking points was generated, and the state library, after being contacted by OELMA, issued a statement of support to fund school librarians in the budget. In July 2009, the bill became law.

What can you learn from Ohio (and the Washington Moms)? Hard, consistent work is the key. Advocacy is an uphill road, and you must be willing to stay in there and fight. Setbacks are likely, but they must not stop you. Whether the activism starts with moms or your state association, partners are needed. No one can do it alone.

Ohio's Evident Success

1. How effective is your state association's advocacy plan?

2. What study has your state association undertaken to substantiate the critical role school librarians play in twenty-first-century learning?

3. Who are some likely partners that will join in supporting your position?

SCANNING THE ENVIRONMENT

The Greek aphorism "Know thyself" is as true today as it was in ancient times. Many prefer not to discover too much about themselves because they do not want to hear unpleasant truths. But as Francis Bacon said, "Knowledge is power," and you cannot afford to be in the dark about the good and the bad in your program. You also need to be constantly on the alert for anything and everything that might have an impact on your SLP.

Assessing Your Program

In chapter 3 you were asked to do an environmental scan, but it was a personal one. At that time, you looked internally at your strengths and weaknesses as a leader. Later you identified the external threats and opportunities, but again this exercise was about *you*. To ensure that the SLP stays in the forefront, you must also assess the environment for your program.

Begin your SWOT (strengths, weaknesses, opportunities, threats) analysis with an internal scan. What does your program do well? What aspects of it are highly regarded and valued? Where is improvement needed? Where has it not met the expectations and needs of your customers and stakeholders? Verify your assessment by asking these questions of teachers, administrators, and students as well as any volunteers, library personnel, or parents. Although it is gratifying to find out where your program is doing well, the areas of weakness are most important to learn. You cannot make adjustments to your program unless you are aware of any perceived lacks.

Because something is a strength does not necessarily mean it must be continued, and not every weakness must be addressed. Both need to be evaluated in terms of time and results. For example, if one of the strengths of the program is extreme accuracy in acquisitions—that is, duplicate copies are never ordered accidentally—you need to weigh the effort needed to do this (checking, rechecking, spreadsheet maintenance, etc.) against saving x number of dollars on a few extra copies in the course of a year. The time spent on maintaining this level of quality control might be better used elsewhere. Conversely, one of the weaknesses of your program might be that books sit on backroom shelves for a while, but you need to determine how much access is lost (you may be letting teachers borrow the titles that are not yet cataloged) and whether higher-priority responsibilities are the cause of the delay.

Few things are black-and-white, and the internal scan is no different. Although you should be aware of whatever you are doing well or poorly, recognize that you cannot do it all. Everything should be subjected to this cost-benefit analysis. Choices must always be made, but they should not be arbitrary or happenstance. Rather you should be assigning priorities to what needs to be continued and what should be changed based on your mission and vision for the SLP.

To do an external scan, look at opportunities and threats. Sometimes the same event can be both. For example, your district is adopting a new instructional model, such as Understanding by Design. If you are among those leading the way, the new program is an opportunity, while it will be a threat if you are not included in the process. In many places, professional learning communities are taking hold. If you are part of them, the other participants will soon be recognizing the value of the SLP. Conversely, if the teachers proceed without you, your program will seem superfluous.

Budget cuts are obvious threats, but you can mitigate their severity if you are ready for them and take a proactive stance. Identify what is essential to the ongoing viability of the SLP, look for ways to cut costs (consider negotiating with vendors and using whatever group purchasing power is available in your state), and, based on the priorities of the program, know what can be eliminated. Take your well-thought-out assessment to your administrator for review. By clearly demonstrating your awareness of the situation and your ability to make wise reductions, you stand a good chance of preserving what is vital while furthering your position as a leader and team player.

Your experiences at the state and national level will also help you be ready to take advantage of any opportunities (government grants and stimulus money) as well as anticipate threats (loss of statewide databases). Although you cannot counter all threats, you will be in far better shape if you know what is coming than if you are suddenly informed of changes. In the first case, you act from a powerful position of knowledge. In the latter one, you are a victim.

SWOT Analysis

1. What is the greatest strength of the SLP?

2. Based on the cost-benefit analysis, should the activity you identified in question 1 continue? Be strengthened further? Reduced?

3. What weaknesses have you identified in the SLP?

4. Which of them must be addressed?

5. Are there any threats that can be turned into opportunities?

Making Larger Connections

As noted earlier, political events on the state and national level very often impact school librarians and their programs, but other happenings in the world at large can play a role—positively or negatively. To take advantage of these or prepare for future challenges, you need to truly scan the environment.

Make it a habit to read the business and science-technology sections of newspapers. If your local paper does not carry much on these topics, go online for the *New York Times* or the *Wall Street Journal* or both. As you learn more about a change in the business world or a new technical development, ask yourself how it might impact education—and the SLP.

Off-shoring and outsourcing have been topics of concern in both business and technology, yet people in education think themselves secure. To them, students need the face-to-face contact that guarantees job security. Although that perception is likely to be the case for some time, the situation could change.

Distance learning is growing in popularity. Some schools are adopting the Singapore system of teaching math. Put all the pieces together, and a new possibility emerges. What if school districts contracted with the best reading or math teachers in the country and had them deliver their lessons via webinars? Only paraprofessionals might be needed to supervise classes. Districts could point to great savings. Lessons could be stored for future replay at home. Sounds like a great idea. Although there are obvious drawbacks to such an approach, it could be presented in a very appealing manner.

What would be the role of the SLP in such a scenario? Would it be possible to have the school librarian's job done remotely? Before you worry too much about the likelihood of that happening, consider whether you could be the distance school librarian if it did.

The purpose of futurecasting is not to alarm you, but rather to keep you mentally agile, flexible, and prepared. The world has been changing fairly rapidly, and you need to be ready to move in new directions or risk getting left behind. Some of these possibilities should also suggest new partners and different approaches for your advocacy.

Another example from the headlines is Microsoft's new multitouch computer that looks like a tabletop (www.microsoft.com/surface). Although it will be a few years before the device is widespread, you can be sure that it is on the way. What could that mean if you were planning a renovation of your school library? How could you leverage this information to create a state-of-the-art facility?

Whatever you see, hear, and read needs to be interpreted through the filter of the SLP. It is not paranoid; it is farseeing. Students need to become global citizens because society is now interconnected. You must raise your awareness of this outside world, because it is *not* out there somewhere beyond your walls, it is entering your environment every day. Be ready for it.

Scanning the Outside World

1. How often do you read business and technology news reports?

2. Find one business article and make a connection from it to your program.

3. Find one technology article and do the same.

4. What other section of the newspaper (other than the political scene) might suggest a future impact on the SLP?

KEY IDEAS

- Economic issues and political actions on the state and national levels can have a direct impact on your district and your position.
- To be prepared for the potential effect of these issues and actions, you need to participate in your state and national organizations.
- Join your state association and become an active member.
- Let your principal know what benefits to the school and students will result from your conference attendance.
- Plan to present a program at your state conference.
- Join a committee and consider running for office.
- Being aware of state happenings gives you advance warning of potential challenges, and *you* may be the one who notifies your administrators about them.
- Explore the three national organizations that relate to the SLP and join at least one.

- AASL is the only national organization focused exclusively on the role of the school librarian and is responsible for developing national standards for the SLP.
- Volunteer to serve on national committees in person or virtually.
- You speak with greater authority and fluency on issues regarding the profession as a result of serving on the state and national levels.
- Learn how to court government officials and participate in legislative days in your state and as part of ALA's National Library Legislative Day.
- Respond to requests to contact your legislators when important bills are pending.
- The Washington Moms are an example of a parent-organized, successful grassroots advocacy campaign in support of school librarians and their programs.
- The Ohio Plan demonstrates the effectiveness of a state association and its partners in creating an advocacy strategy that strengthened SLPs after the legislature planned cuts.
- The Washington Moms and the Ohio Plan were successful because the people involved persevered despite setbacks, learning all the while.
- Advocacy strategies must maintain a positive focus and not be defensive or attack anyone.
- Assess your program's strengths and weaknesses to determine what changes, if any, need to be made.
- Scan the outside world for potential opportunities for and threats to the SLP.
- Become aware of developments in business and technology and envision how these might impact the SLP.

Notes

1. www.aasl.org/ala/mgrps/divs/aasl/aboutaasl/essential/essentialfunctions.cfm
2. www.ala.org/ala/issuesadvocacy/advocacy/federallegislation/getinvolved/index.cfm
3. www.ala.org/ala/newspresscenter/news/pressreleases2009/november2009/hrskillsact_piowo.cfm
4. D. L. Whelan, "Three Spokane Moms Save Their School Libraries" (electronic version), *School Library Journal* 54 (2008): 9.
5. www.infohio.org/12-13TransitionWhitePaper200809.pdf

CHAPTER 10
Does This Really Work?

I'm almost finished reading, but I still haven't spotted the guarantee.

By now you have gone through an extensive look at yourself and your program. You identified a host of stakeholders, some of whom you never previously considered. You are probably wondering how you will ever include all the new tasks and responsibilities that go along with advocacy and leadership when you already have a challenging, complex (but wonderful) job that demands all your time and attention. Meanwhile a nagging voice in the back of your head keeps asking, "Even if I manage to do all these things, will it work?"

REALITY CHECK

The answer to that persistent question is yes, it will work, but not in every case and not all the time. There are few guarantees in life. You cannot control other people or events. You can only control your own actions, behaviors, and attitudes.

However, the corollary is this: if you ignore the recommendations and focus on doing the best job you can, *solely* within the confines of the school library, you are putting your job and program in jeopardy. Gone are the days when school personnel were hired in the way that one would purchase furniture and supplies. In the past, when a new school was opened, the administrators would put the requisite number of desks and chairs in classrooms and, in the same way, stock the building with the appropriate number of teachers, nurses, guidance staff, school librarians, paraprofessionals, clerks, and secretaries. The numbers would vary by the size of the school and the district's view of the correct proportion of staff to students, but the overall pattern was the same. Once the school opened, staffing remained relatively constant. If the student population increased, additional teachers might be hired, but overall changes in personnel were only a matter of replacing those who left.

Several factors have altered this landscape completely. Economic downturns have forced hard decisions on local school districts. State and federal funding continues to shrink while other costs rise. Keeping up with technology has siphoned off large amounts of budget dollars. Before 1995, a medium-sized district might have had one person responsible for A/V. That person took on the first computers as well, but the job soon got far too big. Now there are whole departments in just about every location with all the associated equipment and salaries. In addition, computer teachers have been added to the staff.

Concerns about students being able to function in a global economy have meant that world languages are being introduced at younger grades, resulting in the hiring of more teachers while fewer dollars are available. Not only are subjects such as Mandarin Chinese becoming standard offerings, but graduation requirements are being raised to include more years of language study.

Federal mandates and increased testing have focused attention on certain subject areas, causing the neglect of others. It has become an axiom that "what gets tested gets funded." The flip is that subjects (including the SLP, which is not technically a subject) that are not tested lose funds.

With so many demands placed on ever-fewer budget dollars, you must stand out or be lost in the shuffle. You now have the tools to ensure that your role is regarded as vital by stakeholders within and outside the school. In *most* cases this backing will ensure that your program will continue and be supported to the best level the district can manage. (In other words, some cuts are likely when things get very bad.) However, there are times when nothing you do is enough. You need to be prepared for that eventuality as well.

No Money-Back Guarantees

1. What areas or subjects seem to be protected from cuts in your district?

2. Does your program provide value to these areas and subjects?

3. Where have you begun to show your leadership—or expanded on what you have previously done?

HONEST ASSESSMENT

As you should do with any program or project, you need to assess to what extent your strategic plan was successful. At the completion of any component, you look at what worked and what did not and determine if anything should be done differently either immediately or in the future.

Whether or not you do these interim assessments, you must look at the plan as a whole when the school year concludes. Wait till classes are over. Either come in the next day or even a week later. You need uninterrupted quiet to reflect, revise, and set your goals for the next year.

Did you complete all you set out to do? To what extent did your plans turn out the way you expected? What obstacles did you encounter? What achievements can you celebrate? Do not overlook this part. It is important to recognize what you did well. Focusing only on what did not work gives as false a picture as looking only at success.

Analyze whether your successes moved you forward. Sometimes a plan works, but you do not get the anticipated results. For example, you might have had a collaboration goal and did work with the targeted teachers, but none of them returned for another unit. Perhaps you did not include an assessment with them at the conclusion—one part of which would be to look at what could be done next to further the learning that occurred. Possibly, once the lesson was over, you were so busy with other tasks you did not follow up with more suggestions.

If some of your plans never came to fruition or did not go the way you wanted, look closely to see what happened. Remember, we are in a relationship business. If you have not developed a trusting connection, communication tends to become uncertain. You are not informed about details and changes. The point is not to blame yourself for what went awry but rather to look at the situations honestly and see what you can learn from them going forward.

Now is the time for you to set your goals and action plans for next year. Based on your assessment, your mission and vision, and any changes that have occurred in the district since you created your strategic plan (which includes the advocacy component), determine what you want to accomplish next. You now have a better sense of what can and cannot be achieved in the amount of time you have. Build on what worked. Focus on a cost-benefit approach (i.e., what will give you the biggest return for the time and effort you will invest).

Enter plans onto your spreadsheet. Indicate what you have completed either by using the highlight feature or by making a column where you can check the item off. Having a visual reminder of what you achieved will energize you as you begin once again in the fall.

Reaping the Rewards

1. What were your biggest successes?

2. How have they furthered your position as a leader and strengthened the SLP?

3. What did you learn from what did not work?

4. What is the one big thing you want to accomplish next year?

A VITAL SKILL

Many of the skills necessary for becoming indispensable you already have. Most school librarians work well with others, are flexible, and are lifelong learners. However, there is one skill that few have honed, and even those who have it do not necessarily act on it, yet it is critical for your survival.

Every school librarian needs to be able to read the handwriting on the wall and be prepared to make decisions based on it. Despite all your hard work on advocacy and being a building leader, circumstances can lead to the elimination of your job or serious changes to it. Waiting to discover whether your assessment was correct can be a costly mistake.

In one case, a supportive superintendent of schools announced she was retiring in two years. A high school librarian analyzed the situation and realized that the principal who had always thrown up obstacles to the SLP would be more powerful and within a few years could become superintendent. The school librarian immediately began what was a successful job search. Her concerns proved justified. Teachers with whom she stayed in contact reported that in very short order things changed for the worse. By the time the school librarian had tenure in her new location, her old principal was the superintendent. The staff and the budget for the school library had been severely reduced, and the program had deteriorated drastically.

A more serious scenario occurred in a larger district where a supervisor with a library degree retired. One school librarian assessed the situation and felt certain that an assistant superintendent who had never liked that supervisor would now find it easy to eliminate school librarian positions. In anticipation of what she thought would happen, she took a job in another district. Four years later, all the elementary school librarians were terminated. Surely at least a few of them suspected this turn of events might occur, but rather than risk losing tenure (and their sick days) they remained where they were, hoping they were wrong.

Whenever new administrators arrive in the district, you need to determine whether they present a threat or an opportunity. In most cases, by using your leadership skills and being proactive in demonstrating how the SLP can advance their vision, the transition is an opportunity. But you must always be mindful that you are starting from scratch. You have no history with a new person and must prove yourself all over again.

Recognize that administrators show up with preconceived notions about school librarians and their value to a school or district based on those administrators' previous experience. Unless they worked with school librarians who were building leaders, they are not likely to think too highly of you or your program. Do some checking and find out the degree to which they supported SLPs in the past.

If you do not like what you learn, consider the alternatives. One or two meetings will reveal whether it is possible to win over this administrator. If you feel that is not going to happen, trust your reaction, and then decide what you will do next. Your position may remain secure only until that administrator is comfortable enough to take action. What is the bigger risk—staying where you are or finding a new job?

Even when a principal or superintendent does not plan to eliminate school librarian positions, is he or she likely to drastically cut your budget? Change your schedule? Add classes? Assign extra duties? Move special classes into the school library? Is the new person technology-shy and not willing to invest money in staying current? Any of those situations will affect how well you can serve the needs of students and teachers. Are you willing to spend years under such constraints?

Do not let fear of the unknown keep you from acting on the evidence. Not making a choice is a choice. Take charge of your career. You never want to let your working environment rob you of your passion for what you do.

It Is on the Wall

1. Have you ever had to prove yourself to a new administrator? What worked? What did not?

2. Under what circumstances would you consider leaving your position?

3. What might keep you from following your instincts?

MANAGING STRESS

Considering the first three sections of this chapter as well as what has been discussed earlier, your stress level probably has been rising. Recognizing and dealing with stress is crucial for a number of reasons. Stress will affect your attitude, which then sends those negative nonverbal messages. It is also an energy-waster, and you need all your strength to do the job students and teachers deserve. Finally, there is a link between stress and physical well-being. You do not want to compromise your immune system because of your work.

Look at the sources of your stress. Teachers, students, administrators, technology (or the technology department), or other stakeholders may be putting pressure on you. The scope and responsibilities of your job may be another cause.

To develop a far more calm approach to your daily life, start by making an honest assessment of what you realistically can do in a day, week, marking period, or whatever unit of time works best for you. Look at the list you created and decide what is feasible and what is not. Cut out what you feel you cannot do—just be sure you are not eliminating key elements of your strategic plan.

Next, put your list in priority order. Include *all* your priorities. Some people say that their family is most important to them and then behave quite differently. If you are staying late every night, you are not putting that relationship first.

Do not eliminate or avoid a task because you dislike it. If you know it must be done, it will prey on your mind and add to your stress. Doing it first may be the best solution, as that will remove the task from your list and you will not be constantly staring at it.

Look for help. You have developed relationships—now use them. If you do too many favors for people without asking them to return one or two, they become uncomfortable with a built-up bank of obligations. Consider the request in another way. You like helping others; do not deprive them of the same opportunity. Perhaps someone has a suggestion that will lessen the task. You never know unless you ask.

One reason you are overwhelmed is that you are doing things alone. That tends to make you feel as though you are pulling more than your share of the load. Martyrs are never fun to have as partners.

Remind yourself often that what you are doing is not a matter of life or death. Are you setting artificial deadlines? Often, you then act as though these are real and the world will collapse if you do not get the tasks done "on time."

Find the fun in what you are doing. Learn to laugh at the idiocies that occur in the course of your day. No day should be complete without learning something new and having a good laugh. Both lighten the spirit.

Identify your calming techniques. Can you meditate or do deep breathing? Does a walk clear your head? Does taking time to read for pleasure refresh you? Have you tried yoga? Bubble baths? Going to a movie with a friend? If you do not schedule time to destress, you will explode.

One of the best ways to develop a better perspective is to get a new job. No, this does not mean leaving the one you have. Volunteer for some community project or with a nonprofit. In giving back to others, somehow your own problems dwindle in size, and you feel better about yourself.

SOS—Stamp Out Stress

1. How do you behave when you are under stress?
2. What have been the consequences of your working when highly stressed?
3. Which of the suggestions will be of most help?
4. How often will you schedule them into your workweek?
5. How often do you laugh in the course of the day?

PARTNERSHIP FOR 21ST-CENTURY SKILLS

In chapter 2, NETS-S and NETS-T were suggested as means of establishing your leadership. NETS-A was recommended as a topic for a conversation with your superintendent in chapter 4. Another nonlibrary set of "standards" can substantially increase your value and visibility if you know how to leverage it. The Partnership for 21st Century Skills (P21; www.p21.org) consists of thirty-eight companies and associations in education, business, and technology. Members include AASL, ASCD, NEA, Adobe, Ford Motor Company, LEGO Group, Dell,

Microsoft, Sesame Workshop, and Verizon, among others. The combination gets attention from administrators and other stakeholders.

The Partnership has developed a Framework for 21st Century Learning that defines twenty-first-century skills. Although not truly a statement of standards, the Framework details a direction for the future and, if you know how to present it, furthers the role of the SLP. Although information literacy skills are only one small part of the Framework, closer examination quickly reveals that the SLP and AASL's *Standards for the 21st-Century Learner* must play an active role for this new view of education to come to fruition.

Composed of a double arch and four ripples, the colorful Framework graphic is a visual description of where the curriculum must go if students are to be competitive in a twenty-first-century economy.

The green inner arch is devoted to Core Subjects and 21st-Century Themes. The subjects are:

- English, reading, or language arts
- World languages
- Arts
- Mathematics
- Economics
- Science
- Geography
- History
- Government and civics

What make this list twenty-first-century are the five themes (global awareness; financial, economic, business, and entrepreneurial literacy; civic literacy; health literacy; and environmental literacy). These themes must be interwoven throughout all the subjects.

The outer arch is composed of three parts: Life and Career Skills; Learning and Innovation Skills; and Information, Media, and Technology Skills. (The last includes information literacy; media literacy; and ICT, or information and communications technologies, literacy.) The descriptors under the first two parts, along with the first theme, strongly resemble what is in the AASL Standards and in NETS-S. Here is where you will see recognition for the importance of creativity and innovation, flexibility and adaptability, initiative and self-direction, critical thinking and problem solving, and communication and collaboration.

The four ripples address the structure necessary to carry out this educational view. In addition to Standards and Assessments and Curriculum and Instruction, the Framework includes Professional Development and Learning Environments. The last category includes the human and physical support required to further the development of professional learning communities and the design elements needed to allow twenty-first-century learning to occur.

Check out Route 21, which offers one-stop shopping for supporting resources and information, including lesson plans and websites. Search here for the ICT Literacy Maps, now complete for several subject areas. Before sharing the maps with teachers and administrators, identify where the SLP can contribute to the described learning. Click on "21st Century Skills" for downloadable definitions that will help you better understand the Framework.

A number of states have already joined P21, and more are bound to come on board in the next few years. If your state is not yet part of P21, stay on the alert so that you know as soon as your governor elects to join. Your state library association needs to be part of any organizing task force and subsequent advisory board.

Even if your state is not making any plans to join P21, bring the Framework—and the list of partners—to your administrators. You want to open a dialogue on how to restructure the curriculum at all grades and in all subjects so that it is truly preparing students for their future.

Working with the Partnership

1. Which subjects or themes in any of the arches surprised you?
2. Who do you think will be most interested in the Framework?
3. How will you bring P21 to your administrators?
4. What can you do with the ICT Literacy Maps?
5. What learning environments need to change in your school for twenty-first-century learning to occur?

NATIONAL BOARD CERTIFICATION

If you really want to proclaim your mastery as a professional, there is no better way than to work toward National Board Certification. Although the procedure is daunting, those who have gone through it and been certified attest to the professional growth they have experienced in completing the process.

The National Board for Professional Teaching Standards (NBPTS) has twenty-five certification areas. All have common elements plus specifics that apply to individual subject disciplines. The certification for Library Media/Early Childhood through Young Adulthood is no exception.

A thirteen-page overview of the assessment explains how you demonstrate your abilities as a teacher and your content knowledge of the subject.[1] Just looking at the ten standards for the certification is an excellent reminder of what is involved in being an exemplary school librarian. These standards are divided into three categories: What Library Media Specialists Know; What Library Media Specialists Do; and How Library Media Specialists Grow as Professionals.

You will have to submit four portfolios: one with samples of student work; two with videos of you interacting with students; and one showing your contributions outside the school and the impact these have on student learning. As you can imagine, developing these four portfolios takes a great deal of time, introspection, analysis, and hard work.

In addition to preparing the portfolios, you must perform six exercises at the assessment center and are given up to thirty minutes for each. These exercises demonstrate (1) your content knowledge and understanding of administering the school library, (2) your recognition of what is needed to deal with challenges, (3) your knowledge of hardware and software necessary to implement a program, (4) your ability to assess a collection, (5) your comprehension of the components of information literacy, and (6) your awareness of children's or young adult literature and how it can be utilized within a content area. Samples of the exercises are given so you can get an idea of what is involved.

Once you decide to work toward certification, look for resources to help you through the process. Find out which school librarians in your state have earned certification and ask one of them to be your mentor. Many states have scholarships and other assistance to fund those seeking to become certified because the process involves a significant expense. On the other hand, some districts and states offer financial incentives to those who hold certification, attesting to how highly it is valued.

Find out if your state library association offers any support. Programs are sometimes presented at conferences by those who have successfully gone through the process. Invest in Gail Dickinson's *Achieving National Board Certification for School Library Media Specialists: A Study Guide* (ALA Editions, 2005). As someone who was involved in the NBPTS certification for school librarians from the beginning and has given many workshops on the subject, Dickinson is preeminently qualified to guide you through the steps, making the process much less intimidating.

If you have several years' experience in the profession and your retirement is not imminent, investing in yourself by working toward NBPTS certification is a worthwhile project. The recognition you achieve at the end is nothing compared to the learning that is part of the journey. When districts take a hard look at staffing with an eye toward making cuts, you want to use every resource at your disposal to stand out from the crowd and attest to your value.

On Board with Board Certification

1. What is one good reason for you to seek NBPTS certification?

2. How many school librarians in your state are Board certified?

3. What resources are offered by your state library association to those working toward the certificate?

4. What financial aid can you get?

FINAL WORDS

From focusing on yourself at a personal level to developing a national view not only of school librarianship but of the global society in which you work, you have seen how every day is another opportunity to become a better advocate for the SLP and ready students for a successful future. What remains are a few unpleasant realities about your colleagues that affect how you are perceived by others, and some final reminders of why you chose this career. Both bring this volume to a close as a reminder that it is always necessary to take a realistic view of the world while retaining a sense of optimism that attracts supporters to your cause.

Unfortunate Truths

One of the rarely discussed truths is that the negative attitudes of administrators, teachers, students, and parents are often caused by unfortunate encounters with school librarians. Most people have experiences with only a few school librarians, so these "examples" become the image that key stakeholders have about the role, behavior, and attitude of school librarians in general. In essence, your colleagues may be your worst enemies.

Every time a school librarian says no to a teacher for almost any reason, the message is that *all* school librarians are unwilling to be helpful in a pinch. If rules become more important than service, students have no interest in spending more time than they must in the school library. When parents run a book fair in the school library and the school librarian disappears, they see little connection between the SLP and literacy. Worst of all is a school librarian who tells an administrator, "That's not *my* job." If it needs to be done, and someone else steps up to do it, the school librarian is labeled lazy and not a team player.

Be extra cautious not to send any of these messages. Your reputation can be damaged very quickly. Listen to what your colleagues say at staff development days. If you hear comments that can negatively affect perceptions of the SLP, consider discussing the issue when you meet with the other school librarians.

(You should be getting together on a monthly basis to stay aware of what is happening throughout the district.)

People who focus on obstacles become enamored of their problems. You want to help your colleagues develop positive images of the program. Suggest at your district meeting that all problems be brought with the understanding that possible solutions will be offered. On an altruistic level, you certainly want school librarians to be well regarded, but you also have a stake in one another's personal success. The best incentive for maintaining an active SLP is for *all* of you to be recognized as indispensable.

Teacher burnout is often used as an argument against tenure, but, once again, because of the ratio of school librarians to the total faculty, when school librarians burn out, the results are even more critical. No matter how justified their complaints, those who whine about aspects of their job situation are soon discouraged about everything. Because personality is such a significant factor in the success of the SLP, their attitude begins a downward spiral. They become apathetic, unwilling to be innovative or creative. They become short tempered, and usually students are the recipients of their unhappiness. If someone can intervene early, some behavioral changes might be made and the direction of that spiral could be reversed. The difficult truth is that it would be best for such people to look for an alternate career. Their level of unhappiness and negativity is likely to affect their health adversely, and their interactions with students and staff will surely create negative perceptions about school librarians and the SLP.

Although *you* do not fall into this category, learn to watch your words carefully. Never say that something—or someone—is a problem. Speak in terms of challenges and opportunities. Your language will affect your own approach to dealing with the situation and not project a negative attitude. In the school environment, if you are someone with a lot of problems, you have become the problem.

Watching Your Back

1. Are there school librarians in your district who seem to always complain?

2. Can you come up with a strategy to help them see how they are hurting their position (and yours)?

3. What challenges do you face and what might be done to turn them into opportunities?

Back to the Beginning

While putting your energies to work on your advocacy strategy, never forget a frequently overlooked truism—people like libraries. They like public libraries and school libraries. Legislators love getting awards from libraries because they do not carry any negative baggage. No one really wants to eliminate libraries or reduce their capabilities to offer services.

Cuts occur because of a combination of indifference and misunderstandings. There are many versions of the Edmund Burke quotation "All that is necessary for the triumph of evil is for good men to do nothing," but the essence of the words is that danger comes from inaction—which is often the result of indifference. Despite the warm, fuzzy thoughts libraries inspire, few people are *passionate* defenders of them.

There is an assumption (hence the misunderstanding) that somehow what is liked about libraries will be taken care of through other means. In schools, the belief is that the classroom or computer teacher can minimize the loss of the school librarian. Besides, many think the school library *is* the program, so if the doors are open, even if the facility is staffed by clerks or volunteers, students' needs will be met.

Your job is to move stakeholders from indifference to action and be sure that no one can hide behind misconceptions. Go back to chapter 1. Review the three areas you said were unique to the SLP. Be sure everyone is aware of them. You can be eliminated, but you cannot be replaced.

Reread your mission statement and tagline. Have you fully proclaimed your purpose? Does your tagline need to be jazzed up to make it more memorable? Now that you have explored so many aspects of advocacy and leadership, you may want to tweak both your mission statement and tagline to make them as powerful as possible.

Review the vision statement you created in chapter 2. Does it make you proud of what you are committed to achieving? Make changes if you think it can be more compelling. Refer to it regularly. No matter what the day or the world throws at you, your vision statement will empower you and keep you enthusiastic about being in one of the most exciting professions and making a difference in students' lives!

Uniquely You

1. Do you need to add to the unique contributions you make to students' learning?

2. Rewrite your mission statement with the changes.

_____

3. What is your improved tagline?

_____

4. Which words of your vision inspire *you*?

_____

KEY IDEAS

- Because of situations completely outside your control, even the best advocacy strategy cannot guarantee that your program will not be cut or eliminated.
- Look at your entire strategic plan at the end of the year and reflect, assess, and revise.
- Learn to read the handwriting on the wall and be prepared to act accordingly.
- Stress is a constant in today's world. Use a variety of approaches to minimize its effect on you.
- Become familiar with the website of the Partnership for 21st Century Skills and share it with all relevant stakeholders.
- Investigate the possibility of seeking National Board Certification to further solidify your position as an exemplary teacher and school librarian.
- Be aware of your school librarian colleagues whose negativity can be affecting stakeholders' perceptions of the district's SLP.
- Review and tweak your mission statement and tagline.
- Hold onto your vision and let it remind you that you make a difference in the lives of students *every day*.

Note

1. National Board for Professional Teaching Standards, *Library Media/Early Childhood through Young Adulthood: Assessment at a Glance,* www.nbpts.org/userfiles/File/ECYA_LM_AssessAtaGlance.pdf.

APPENDIX
Web Resources

Some of the following have been mentioned in the various chapters. Others are additional sites that are relevant.

ANNOTATED SOURCES

AASL Crisis Toolkit: www.ala.org/ala/mgrps/divs/aasl/aaslissues/toolkits/crisis.cfm. Resources to help when your program is either being cut or eliminated.

AASL Essential Links: Resources for School Library Media Program Development: http://aasl.ala.org/essentiallinks/index.php?title=Main _Page. An A–Z wiki loaded with links.

AASL Learning 4 Life (L4L): National Plan for Implementation of Standards for the 21st-Century Learner and Empowering Learners: Guidelines for School Library Media Programs: www.ala.org/ala/mgrps/divs/aasl/ guidelinesandstandards/learning4life/index.cfm.

AASL Parent Outreach Toolkit: www.ala.org/ala/mgrps/divs/aasl/aaslissues/ toolkits/parentoutreach.cfm. How to connect with parents.

AASL School Library Program Health and Wellness Toolkit: www.ala.org/ ala/mgrps/divs/aasl/aaslissues/toolkits/slmhealthandwellness.cfm. Resources for building an advocacy program.

AASL Standards for the 21st-Century Learner: www.aasl.org/ala/mgrps/divs/ aasl/guidelinesandstandards/learningstandards/AASL_Learning _Standards_2007.pdf. Core document.

ACRL Information Literacy Competency Standards for Higher Education: www.ala.org/ala/mgrps/divs/acrl/standards/ informationliteracycompetency.cfm. Know what college students are expected to be able to do—from the Association of College and Research Libraries.

ALA Intellectual Freedom statements and policies: www.ala.org/ala/ aboutala/offices/oif/statementspols/statementspolicies.cfm. More core documents.

ALSC: School/public library cooperative programs: www.ala.org/ala/mgrps/
     divs/alsc/initiatives/partnerships/coopacts/schoolplcoopprogs.cfm. Ideas
     for outreach.
Education World: http://www.educationworld.com/a_issues/. Loaded with
     information—click on tabs for Administrators, Tech Integration, and
     School Issues to keep up with what is current.
Illinois School Libraries: Information Literacy Wiki: http://
     illinoisschoollibraries.wikispaces.com/Scope+%26+Sequence.
     Locate Information Literacy Curricula and scope and sequence plans
     from several locations.
New Jersey Association of School Librarians (NJASL): Advocacy Wiki: http://
     njasladvocacy.pbworks.com. Check to see if your state has one as well.
Ohio Educational Library Media Association (OELMA): Advocacy: www
     .oelma.org/Advocate_Resources.htm. Another good state site on
     advocacy with talking points and excellent links.
TRAILS: Tools for Real-Time Assessment of Information Literacy Skills:
     www.trails-9.org. If you want to find out what your students need to
     know—and whether they know it.

IMPORTANT NATIONAL ASSOCIATIONS

American Library Association: www.ala.org
American Association of School Librarians: www.aasl.org
Association for Supervision and Curriculum Development: www.ascd.org
Association for Educational Communications and Technology: http://aect.org
International Society for Technology in Education: www.iste.org
Partnership for 21st Century Skills: www.p21.org

RESEARCH STUDIES

Center for International Studies in School Librarianship (CISSL): http://cissl
     .rutgers.edu/
School Library Impact Studies: www.lrs.org/impact.php
School Libraries Work 2008 (Scholastic Publishing): http://www2.scholastic
     .com/content/collateral_resources/pdf/s/slw3_2008.pdf

INDEX

You may also be interested in

 ***New on the Job: A School Library Media Specialist's Guide to Success:*** From job search strategies and discovering your work philosophy to the nitty-gritty details of creating acceptable use policies, this resource serves as a wise mentor for new school library media specialists.

 ***Libraries Got Game: Aligned Learning through Modern Board Games:*** From promoting the idea of designer board games to teachers and administrators to aligning specific games to state and national education standards, this book will help you build a strong collection that speaks to enhanced learning and social development and is just plain fun.

 ***Serving Boys through Readers' Advisory:*** Based on more than twenty years' experience working to get boys interested in reading, Michael Sullivan now offers his first readers' advisory volume. With an emphasis on nonfiction and the boy-friendly categories of genre fiction, the work offers hundreds of suggested titles, booktalks, and lists to help turn boys into rabid readers.

 ***Protecting Intellectual Freedom in Your School Library:*** Tailored to the school library, this title presents a number of scenarios in which intellectual freedom is at risk and includes case studies that provide narrative treatment of common situations arising in school libraries; motivating ways to prepare new hires for handling intellectual freedom issues; sidebars throughout the book that offer sample policies, definitions of key terms, and analysis of important statutes and decisions; and detailed information on how to handle challenges to materials in your collection.